ZERO-BASE BUDGETING

FOR

HEALTH CARE INSTITUTIONS

Ray D. Dillon, D.B.A., C.P.A.

*With a special contribution from
the Alexian Brothers Medical Center
Elk Grove Village, Illinois*

*Bruce Fisher, Vice President-Financial Affairs
and
Dean Grant, Vice President-Operations*

Aspen Systems Corporation
Germantown, Maryland
London, England
1979

Library of Congress Cataloging in Publication Data

Dillon, Ray D.
Zero-base budgeting for health care institutions.

Includes index.

1. Health facilities— Finance.   2. Zero-base
budgeting.   I. Title. [DNLM: 1. Health planning.
2. Cost benefit analysis.   3. Financial management.
4. Health facilities— Economics.   WX157.3 D579z]
RA971.3.D54   658.1'54   79-15046
ISBN 0-89443-150-1

Library of Congress Catalog Card Number: 79-15046
ISBN: 0-89443-150-1

Printed in the United States of America

1 2 3 4 5

To Sue, Chris, and my parents

Table of Contents

Preface

Can anyone deny that health care managers, like managers in corporations or government, face the problem of allocating scarce resources to meet multiple requests? As competition for funds makes them scarcer, the problem becomes more acute. Financial managers constantly seek better ways to decide which projects are most beneficial so they can channel funds in their direction. In health care institutions, where many decisions are made by fiat, weighing the expected benefits—which often are not in terms of cash flow—and the expected costs, managers need a technique to help them make decisions.

Zero-base budgeting (ZBB) provides this much-needed technique. It gives a formalized procedure for establishing the benefits and costs of proposals and for evaluating them against each other so that only the most worthy are funded. The concept has enjoyed widespread publicity in recent years. This notoriety is due, in part, to the election of Jimmy Carter to the Presidency, since he promised to use zero-base in the federal budget. All who speak of zero-base budgeting, and there are a number of books and articles on the subject, have not been complimentary, but the debate over the method's effectiveness is not unhealthy because it has prompted a mitigation of the unfounded virtues some have proposed. Unfortunately, not much of the literature on zero-base budgeting has been directed toward health care institutions. Even though health care financial managers face many of the same problems that confront their corporate and public counterparts, it is difficult to relate the private and public sector solutions to the health care sector.

In 1977, the Hospital Financial Management Association published my paper *Zero-Base Budgeting: An Introduction.* I was encouraged to expand on the subject to provide guidelines for financial managers who might want to implement a system in their hospital, nursing home, or other facility.

This work details the steps to designing and implementing a zero-base system. Also included, at the end of Chapters 1, 2, and 5, are periodical articles that may prove helpful. Appendix A details initial steps toward implementing a zero-base system. Appendix B consists of a report on the case of an important hospital that used zero-base. The case is not intended to illustrate good or bad management practices but to narrate a specific organization's experiences. The health care manager should have an adequate understanding of zero-base budgeting after reading this book. However, experience often is the best teacher, and managers who decide to install zero-base will find their experiences adding to the growing knowledge of the best way to install and operate this budgeting system.

Ray Dillon
Georgia State University
July 1979

Acknowledgments

I would like to thank the editors of *Hospital Financial Management* for allowing me to include material in Chapter 2 from my article on zero-base budgeting published in the November/December 1977 issue. My appreciation also is extended to James Roy, who assisted in acquiring much of the research material, and to Becky Hooten, Marge Authier, and Alice Cummins, who typed the several manuscripts. Above all, I would like to thank my wife, Sue, for her proofing help and her tireless efforts to keep our two-year-old son Chris happily occupied while I worked.

Chapter 1

Budget Overview

THE BUDGET PROCESS

Webster's defines the budget as the annual statement of the probable revenues and expenditures for the following year. An uncomplicated definition, easy to comprehend, but for some health care organizations it is exceedingly difficult to employ effectively. Effective budgeting, whether it be traditional, zero-based budgeting (ZBB), or a combination of both, can add many benefits to the managing of an organization. If applied properly, the budget process can help an inefficient facility lower its costs while maintaining its output or benefits at current levels. It also can increase department heads' awareness and appreciation of the need for intraorganizational communication and coordination of activities. A budget process, properly applied, can help allocate scarce resources away from areas in a health care facility that provide few benefits and move them to areas that will provide greater benefits. The key to receiving the benefits (and there are many more than those mentioned) is *proper application.* This chapter summarizes the basic elements of a properly applied budgeting process so health care financial managers may (1) improve their existing processes, or (2) design and implement systems that will operate effectively from the beginning. This section may be used by the facility administration as a foundation when considering whether to adopt and implement a ZBB system.

THE PLANNING PROCESS

Administrators or budget supervisors tend to begin the budget process by developing the numerical master plan for the coming year. However, before establishing the financial plan, they should allocate time and effort for planning in a nonnumerical sense. The success of the budget process depends largely on the quality of prepreparation planning. Each level of management should be included in this process.

Responsibility for developing plans falls primarily on four levels within the health care institution.

1. the board of directors or trustees
2. the administrator
3. the budget supervisor (often the controller)
4. the firstline supervisor or department head

The governing board is responsible for establishing goals and objectives for the facility. The terms "goals" and "objectives" will have to be defined by each health care facility, but this work limits goal to the long term, while objectives are the points along the paths to goals by which performance and achievement may be judged. Goals and objectives should be defined narrowly; for without some specificity, accomplishments cannot be compared meaningfully with expectations. The administrator is responsible for converting the board's goals and objectives into specific operational plans. Those plans may include service projections, capital expenditures, staffing needs, and fiscal estimations. With such a broad task, the administrator should seek input from others, including the chief financial officer, controller, department heads, and physicians.

The chief fiscal officer (CFO) or controller is responsible for ensuring that the budget preparation procedures are scheduled, routinized, and understood by the individuals responsible. The CFO develops the budget calendar, supplies requested data, consults with department heads as they prepare their operating plans, and assists in consolidating the overall budget to submit for board approval. The CFO is the liaison between the administration's conceptual framework for the health care facility and the operating manager's conversion of the concepts to monetary terms.

Firstline supervisors are responsible for providing the basic operating estimates for their areas. Without their full support and participation in the development of the budget, its effectiveness will be diminished. Since these supervisors will be held responsible for their performance, as judged in part by the comparison of actual costs and revenues to those budgeted, they should be given the authority to develop their own financial plans.

A budget process and timetable appear in Exhibit 1-1. Several characteristics of the planning process are specified or implied in the exhibit. The planning process does not operate without some organizational goals and objectives in mind. Therefore, as the exhibit shows, the planning process begins with a statement of both long- and short-range goals and objectives.

Exhibit 1-1 The Budget Timetable*

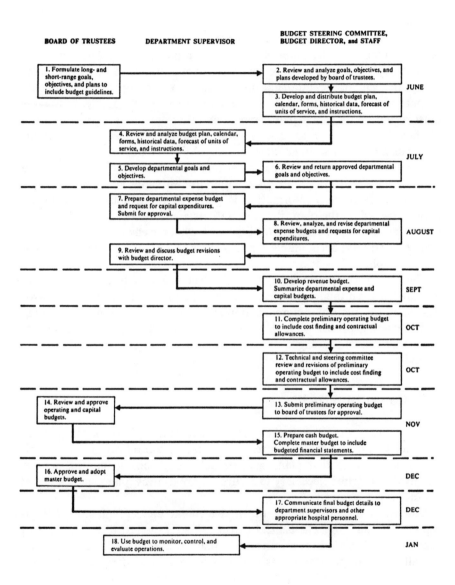

Source: Rate Setting by R. S. Lemer and D. D. Willman. Reprinted by permission of Aspen Systems Corporation, Germantown, Maryland, © 1974.

Since the health care organization often is complex and always dynamic, planning cannot be relegated to a single act during an operating period. Planning is a process and by its nature is continuous; that is, plans prepared today will affect plans made next month, next quarter, and next year. By repeating the planning process continually, managers can meet present objectives and prepare for the dynamic future. Meaningful financial plans cannot be attained fully if managers of operating segments prepare their plans as though their units existed independently. Managers must recognize that their plans impact on other operating segments within the facility, and vice versa. Stated another way, the budget for the organization as a whole is an interactive, not an additive, model.

The administration and department managers must recognize that since planning deals with the future, they must use estimates and forecasts. The implication is that as information is gathered throughout the operating period covered by the plan, the expectations and forecasts should be modified to include new, current data. Even in a dynamic environment, however, managers still are accountable for variations from the plan that are within their control.

The time necessary to develop the budget will vary from institution to institution. Even though the exhibit shows the process as a yearly endeavor beginning six months before its implementation, a continuous planning and budgeting process should be considered. Continuous planning recognizes that current changes will have lasting impacts in the future that should be recognized and anticipated.

THE CONTROL PHASE

If the process ends with the completed financial plans for the current year, a significant budget feature is lost; that is, control over the organizational activities so that plans may be achieved. Control may be defined simply as the action necessary to assure that objectives, plans, policies, and standards are attained.

Control is the last step in the management cycle of planning-acting-reporting-evaluating. The control phase pervades the last three elements of that cycle and these, in turn, affect any plans that may be developed. Plans initially elicit responses or acts undertaken to achieve the goals. The acts have certain quantitative outcomes that managers summarize and report on in a timely manner. The summarization of these results is compared to what was anticipated under the original plan and evaluated so future acts or the plan itself can be modified. The control phase considers whether plans were proper, actions to meet those plans were appropriate, reports were adequate and informative, and the evaluation was objective and focused on the significant problem areas. Generally, the control function follows these steps:

1. measurement and communication of performance to appropriate individuals and groups
2. analysis of deviations of performance from plans in order to isolate causes
3. isolation of alternate decisions that may correct differences between the actual and what was planned
4. selection of the best alternative and implementing it
5. followup on the alternative selected to appraise its effectiveness and use of this information for future planning

PERFORMANCE REPORTING

A performance reporting system is used most often as a means of measuring performance against predetermined plans and communicating this information to appropriate individuals. These reports may take a variety of forms but should disclose, at a minimum, the following:

- the function covered by the report
- the time span the report covers
- the line items the manager can control
- the actual expenditures and revenues by line item for the reporting period
- variances of actual from budget
- relevant statistical data; i.e., procedures delivered, patients treated

Exhibit 1-2 illustrates a typical performance report for a single department. The format should be easy to read and use in evaluating departmental activities.

The performance report brings together the planning and control processes. The variances from budget allow the department manager to exercise the management-by-exception principle. This principle holds that attention should be directed toward the unusual or exceptional items so department managers are not overburdened with details having little or no impact on operations. For example, if a variance from plans is $50 for a given month, the manager, inappropriately or not, may consider it exceptional and, more importantly, take inappropriate action.

The administration should assist the department manager in isolating

Exhibit 1-2 Department Performance Report: February 1980

Department RADIOLOGY

Unit of Service PROCEDURES

Controllable expenses	Month			Year to date		
	Budget	Actual	Variance*	Budget	Actual	Variance*
Salaries and wages	$18,387	$18,949	$(562)(3%)	36,331	37,581	(1250)(3%)
Employee benefits..........	2,332	2,342	(10)(.4%)	4,527	4,646	(119)(2%)
Other expenses	1,231	1,105	126 10%	2,485	2,314	171 7%
Total direct expense	21,950	22,396	(446)(2%)	43,343	44,541	(1198)(3%)
Units of service	588	647	(59)(9%)	1,294	1,353	(59)(4%)
Salaries and wages per unit..............	31.27	29.29	1.98 7%	28.07	27.78	.29 1%
Total direct expenses per unit...............	37.33	34.62	2.71 13%	33.50	32.92	.58 2%

Remarks:

Action:

_____   _____   _____   _____
Initial   Date   Initial   Date

*Favorable (Unfavorable).

exceptional items by establishing policy that will identify exceptional variances for detailed analysis. Lower limits should be set in terms of dollar amounts and relative amounts. Policy should be stated in writing such as: "All variances of $75 or more *or* 10 percent of planned expenditures should be investigated." Policy or the performance report itself should indicate line items the department manager can and cannot control. If no distinction is drawn between these two groups, department managers may perceive improperly that they are held responsible for all variances. Often the result is ill will aimed at the reporting system and the administration.

If policy, rather than the report, defines controllable items for a department, management should send periodic memoranda to all department heads reminding them of line items they are responsible for controlling. If the performance reports distinguish controllable and noncontrollable line items, the reports should label them clearly as such. A performance report that labels items as "Direct" and "Indirect" is inferior to one that labels them "Controllable" and "Noncontrollable."

Many health care organizations tend to focus on the unfavorable variances to the exclusion of favorable variances. Both are important. Unfavorable controllable variances should be analyzed to determine why they occur and modifications should be made to bring the actual in line with the plans. Favorable variances may indicate the use of management methodologies that should be continued. The department manager also should utilize those variances.

Performance reports also should be timely and flexible for maximum usefulness. Timeliness refers to the length of elapsed time between the end of the reporting period and the department head's receipt of the perfor-

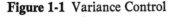

Figure 1-1 Variance Control

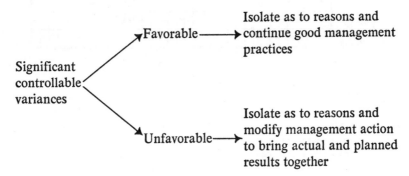

mance report. As time elapses, the usefulness of the data in the report diminishes rapidly until it becomes valueless for decision making. This time-information relationship is shown in Figure 1-2. The length of time between the performance report distribution and the length of time the reporting period ends will vary from facility to facility. A rough guideline would be to limit the time to no more than one-sixth of the reporting period. If the report covers a single month, the elapsed time should be five calendar days or four business days.

Analyzing Deviation from Plans

When analyzing deviations from plans, an institution must use a flexible budget. Many health care facilities have what they believe are flexible budget-

---

Figure 1-2 Relationship of Elapsed Time and Information Value for Performance Reporting

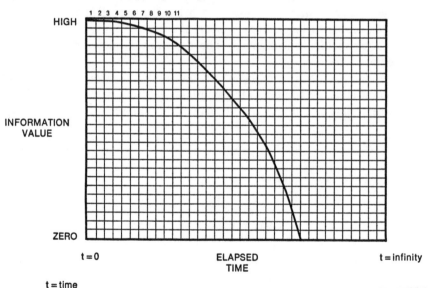

Note: Figure 1-2 illustrates the decline in the information value of performance reports as time elapses between the end of the reporting period and the receipt of the report by the responsible manager. Note that short time elapses have minimal effect on information value but as time passes the decline is severe until the performance report has no information content.

ing systems. Careful study may show the systems actually are not flexible in the true sense of the concept. Flexible budgeting is basic to the control phase. The concept is based on the recognition that some costs will vary with changes in the volume of services provided. The performance report should show the budgeted figure for costs that vary with the amount planned for the level of service achieved for the period. For example, assume that for the line item Medical Supplies, the following appears on the Nursing Unit A performance report for May:

| Line Item | Year-To-Date | | Variance |
	Budget	Actual	F (U)*
Supplies	$10,000	$8,000	$2,000

*Favorable (Unfavorable).

The manager of Unit A would think that is a favorable variance and consider no further investigation is necessary. However, the plans at the beginning of the year estimated $24,000 in supplies would be necessary for an anticipated patient load of 6,000 but, through the month of May, the patient load has been 1,700. The performance report should show:

| Line Item | Year-To-Date | | Variance |
	Budget	Actual	F (U)*
Supplies	$6,800 ($4 × 1,700)	$8,000	($1,200)

*Favorable (Unfavorable).

The unfavorable variance may not be caused by poor management but by a higher average cost per patient. Whatever the reason, the chief nurse of Unit A receives a completely different account of the situation when flexible budgeting is used properly. The $10,000 budget figure in the first report is the planned expenditure ($24,000) divided by 12 months, or $2,000 multiplied by five months (January through May), assuming the fiscal and calendar years are the same.

Flexible budgeting is important in health care institutions even though most of the budgeted costs are inflexible. The reasons include:

- Costs that vary with activity generally are the most susceptible to control in the short run.
- Performance reporting that does not "flex" the budget for activity changes may provide faulty information.
- Faulty information may provoke the department chief to do nothing when action is necessary or to take improper management action.

The performance report should be completed with a written explanation of the causes of the variances and what action is planned. The department head should submit this management action report shortly (perhaps one week) after receipt of the performance report. The department manager is responsible for isolating the reasons for deviations from plans and indicating the steps being taken to correct unfavorable deviations, or for continuing favorable variances.

At this point in the control process, the decision maker should provide the administration with information on permanent changes in the original plans that should be considered for future periods. These include external factors such as competition, changes in physician composition and in the cost of supplies and services, and internal factors, such as wage and salary increases and technical advances. Care should be taken when isolating variations from a particular cause since any action will be deemed appropriate based on a cause that is presumed correct.

Isolating Alternative Actions

Alternative courses of action generally are available for solving a problem, but are isolated when evaluating the performance report. One alternative may be to do nothing and expect a reversal of the problem area. This often is the response to a problem generated by unforeseen environmental effects. This also could include the resignation of a physician or an important staff member, a power shortage, or unseasonably bad weather. Management cannot control these causes, but it can expect that results will come in line with the plans after a period of readjustment. Management should consider the alternatives, select the most appropriate one, and proceed with it. The decision maker should be certain that the alternative selected will solve the problem without creating more difficulties.

Follow-up on the Alternative

One of the more important elements of the decision-making process is the follow-up on the decision. Management should determine whether the decision was appropriate. The only way that can be determined is to decide whether expectations at the time of the selection of the alternative have been achieved. Even though the decision has been made and cannot be changed, the follow-up can provide excellent information for future difficulties of this same nature.

THE BUDGETING PROCESS AND HUMAN BEHAVIOR

The budget is inanimate; it does not live or function by itself. Too often, the budget is referred to as if it had some living power; for example, it is said that "The budget tells us that we are exceeding expected costs," or "If the budget says no more spending, we stop spending." The budget has no such power. It is prepared by people and used by people. Peoples' behaviors are affected by the preparation and use of budgets, but in some cases people are treated as machines, with the budget as a regulator. Perhaps no other financial tool has more impact on the behavior of people in an organization than the budget. Research has shown time and again that behavior is modified when a budget is used. Frequently, this behavior modification is negative; that is, the organization does not benefit from the behavior change. If the administration recognizes the potential problem areas, it can take steps to mitigate or remove the contributing factors. Many behavioral problems are caused by the following:

- lack of acceptance and respect of the budget process by the department head
- inclusion of budgetary slack
- pseudoparticipation
- budget clear-out

A department head's lack of respect for and acceptance of the budget process can pervade an organization and ruin the effectiveness of the budget. This problem stems from two sources:

1. a resistance to something different from what had been experienced previously
2. lack of education in the use and value of financial tools such as the budget for the clinician manager

Almost everyone is resistant to a change in the accustomed environment. The imposition of a budget on an organization that never has had one, or requesting department managers to participate for the first time in the preparation of a budget, or to implement a new system such as zero-base budgeting, are examples of situations where some department heads tend not to accept the change simply because it is a change.

The budget supervisor, with the help of the controller and top management, can relieve most of the resistance problem by following the steps in Exhibit 1-3. These steps are practical and, if followed, will help remove most of the resistance. They are not meant to be comprehensive and, even if followed completely, may not remove all the mistrust or misunderstanding. Human nature is too complex to be dealt with by a few simple steps. However, health care administrators, not unlike top managements in other organizations, have fallen short in two areas:

1. educating those who will be affected most as to the value of the change
2. providing a means of feedback from the bottom level manager up to the administration and providing an understanding (but not necessarily patronizing) person to receive the feedback

Budgetary slack is a universal problem for those administering the process. Slack is a request for unnecessary funding, or a revenue projection lower than might be expected. Either factor can provide the requestor with a "cushion" or slack. Department managers who were asked whether they had included budget slack in their financial plans probably would not recognize the term. However, if they were asked whether they had projected financial needs of their department to be $75,000 for the coming year and would request only $75,000, their response probably would be a uniform, "No, more than $75,000," and they would recognize quickly that budget slack is another name for what they call "padding" or "fat."

Budget supervisors have few means of reducing or eliminating budget slack. The major difficulty is the isolation of budget slack from the funding necessary for operations. The budget supervisor, the controller, and their staffs would be required to know intimately every program under the administrator and the amount of funding necessary for each.

Before anything can be accomplished on budget slack, the question of why it occurs at all must be answered. There are several reasons, but two seem to be most common. The first is the belief—shared by many department heads—that if they are over budget, their performance will be rated poorly, primarily because of the budget overruns. Poor performance ratings may mean reprisals ranging from administrative reprimands to relief

Exhibit 1-3 Initiating Change in an Organization

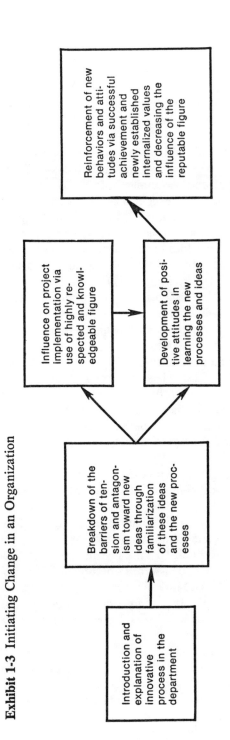

Source: Zero-Base Budgeting—A New Home in the Federal Government by P. M. J. Reckers and Donna Ritchik. Reprinted by permission of the Association of Government Accountants. © 1977.

from administrative duties or, perhaps worse, an appearance of managers' inadequacy before their peers. The second is almost as frequent and many more times inexcusable. As one person expressed it, "I am forced to put slack in my budget. When I submit my budget, the controller cuts it by 10 percent; therefore, I add 10 percent before I submit it and we are both happy."

A natural question is: who started this game—the controller or the department chief. If the controller began it, not much time passed before the department chief recognized it and the budget game was on. If the department chief initiated the process, the controller is not handling it properly if the two had no dialogue to clear it up. To solve these two problem causes (slack is only a symptom of a disease), the budget supervisor and the administrator should point out that the performance report is only one source of management appraisal and perhaps not the most important. Those responsible for operating under the budget also should be given an opportunity to explain any unfavorable variances and management should accept an adequate explanation. The budget supervisor must avoid arbitrary fund-cutting because, although department heads may not be fully educated in the uses of financial tools, they are not stupid.

Even these steps may not eliminate slack entirely, but small reductions can make significant cost cuts. Budgetary slack results in a misallocation of resources. Assume a small hospital has a budget of $2 million, but this includes 10 percent slack. If slack can be reduced 1 percent, there is a saving of $20,000 that can be put into other projects or used to reduce the cost of patient care. Clearly, the attempt to reduce slack, if approached properly, is worth the effort.

The term pseudoparticipation implies the problem. The difficulty manifests itself in many ways, but the most common may be exemplified by the situation where the chief of radiology devotes great time and effort to budget preparation. The budget supervisor sends back a final budget that has little or no similarity to the one submitted. A request for an explanation of the vast differences is answered: "That's just how it all worked out; it's technical accounting you really don't want to become involved in." After a reply like that, the chief will spend little time on next year's financial plan or have little regard for this year's. If participation is sought, it must be utilized. Better an authoritarian budget handed down than a budget falsely using participation.

Budget clearing, which may be an inappropriate phrase, involves the difference between actual and planned expenditures. If the actual is less, the difference is spent, so the amount is cleared out to zero or near zero. There may be nothing improper about this procedure, for the budget is a plan for funds to be spent as well as a limit on the amount. That is, if $10,000 is to be spent on continuing education and only $5,000 actually is expended, there may be long-range dysfunctional consequences if therapists are not kept up to date on the latest procedures and modalities. However, if funds are being expended at fiscal year-end simply to avoid having to return unused amounts, a behavioral problem exists. If department managers were asked why they spend the funds at year-end, they probably would respond unanimously: "If we don't spend it, we don't get it back next year because the administration will assume we don't need the funds."

The solution to the problem of spending unused and unneeded funds can be approached in two ways:

1. Management should have an understanding with department heads that their budgets will not be cut back for two years, even if they do not use all the resources allocated to them.
2. Management, in a stance similar to the first, announces that subsequent budgets will not be tied directly to previous years. It will state that each budget stands alone and must be justified individually from zero. If funding can be justified and funds are available, they will be allocated to the department.

SUMMARY

This overview of the budgeting process covers two distinct phases: planning and control. One cannot exist without the other. Emphasizing one phase to the partial exclusion of the other is unwise and has far-reaching negative implications. Common problems that may arise in any budgeting context also have been examined. While these problems are common in traditional budgeting, they also can occur when zero-base budgeting is applied. The problems discussed centered on the behavior of people. The primary cause of these problems is the administration's implicit view of its subordinates as machines and not human beings.

To some health care administrators, the budget is a regulating device or a gauge to tell whether or not a machine is operating properly. Department heads must be worked with as individuals, with individual problems. They should be given an opportunity to plan and carry out those plans. In recent times, this planning process has been enhanced greatly by Zero-Base Budgeting (ZBB). The next chapters will discuss the purpose and implementation of ZBB.

Reading

MURPHY'S LAW VS. ZERO-BASE BUDGETING*

by Donald N. Anderson

**"Research" by a zero-base advocate shows how the famous
Ralph Murphy was miles ahead of Peter Pyhrr.**

Widespread interest in zero-base budgeting has led apostles and practitioners alike to expound on how this management process works. Since the initial exposure of the concept by Peter Pyhrr in a *Harvard Business Review* article in 1970 and in his book three years later, many other articles and several books have explored the mechanics, the virtues, and the hazards of implementing what is really a sound, fundamental system of management discipline.

This extensive body of literature on the subject indicates that zero-base is no longer a fad; it has become a culture unto itself. The potential applications of the zero-base technique range from an individual householder's spending plans to the programs and projects of industry, schools, churches, and government at all levels. One spokesman with a horticultural bent even asserts that the process can be used to eliminate "corporate crabgrass."

My survey of the literature on zero-base budgeting leads me to conclude that a grave injustice has been heaped upon one of the earliest pioneers in the development of management systems, including zero-base: Ralph Murphy. Ralph was a pragmatist, an experienced administrator as well as a staff specialist. I understand he also dabbled in the laboratory sciences and in applied engineering; some of his earliest enunciations of "Murphy's Law" appeared in electronic and aerospace journals.

However, the full impact of his work in management systems is not generally appreciated. In posthumous recognition of the genius of Ralph

---

*Reprinted, by permission of the publisher, from *Management Review*, October 1977, © 1977, by AMACOM, a division of American Management Associations. All rights reserved.

Murphy, I have taken it upon my shoulders to transcribe verbatim his laws and rules concerning the implementation of management systems exactly as they were found in his original, tear-stained, handwritten manuscripts. The full significance of his four laws and six rules, which were ignored for years, becomes blisteringly clear in the heat of passion for zero-base budgeting.

Murphy's Laws for Implementation of Planning and Budgeting Systems

First Law: In any field of public or private endeavor, anything that can go wrong *will* go wrong.

Corollary 1: Everything goes wrong at one time.

Corollary 2: If there is a possibility of several things going wrong, the one that will go wrong is the one that will do the most damage.

Corollary 3: Left to themselves, things will always go from bad to worse.

Corollary 4: Plans must be reproducible; they should fail in the same way.

Corollary 5: Nature always sides with the hidden flaw.

Corollary 6: If everything seems to be going well, you have overlooked something.

Second Law: It is usually impractical to worry beforehand about interference during system implementation; if you have none, someone will supply it for you.

Corollary 1: Information necessitating a change in plans will be conveyed to you after, and only after, the plans are complete.

Corollary 2: In listing alternatives, presenting one obvious right way versus one obvious wrong way, it is often wiser to choose the wrong way to expedite subsequent revisions.

Corollary 3: The more innocuous a modification appears to be, the further its influence will extend and the more plans will have to be redrawn.

Third Law: In any collection of performance and accounting data, the figures that are obviously correct and beyond all need of checking contain the errors.

Corollary 1: Those you ask for help will not see the error.

Corollary 2: Any nagging intruder who stops by with unsought advice will spot it immediately.

Fourth Law: If in any problem situation you find yourself doing an immense amount of work, the answer can be obtained by simple inspection.

Murphy's Rules for Effective Use of
Planning and Budgeting Systems

Rule 1: Prepare no plans or proposals simply if a way can be found to make them complex and wonderful.

Rule 2: A detailed compilation of data is useful; it indicates that you have been busy.

Rule 3: Before studying a subject, first understand it thoroughly.

Rule 4: Do not believe in luck; rely on it.

Rule 5: Always leave room, when writing a variance report, to add another explanation if the first one does not work (Rule of the Way Out).

Rule 6: Always use the most recent developments in the field of interpretation of budgeting variances:

—Items such as Finagle's Constant and the more subtle Bougerre Factor are loosely grouped in business mathematics under constant variables or, if you prefer, variable constants.

—Finagle's Constant, a multiplier of the zero-order term, may be characterized as changing the budget to fit the recorded figures.

—The Bougerre Factor is characterized as changing the recorded figures to fit the budget. It is also known as the "Soothing Factor"; mathematically similar to the damping factor, it has the characteristic of dropping the subject variance under discussion to zero.

—A combination of the two, the Diddle Coefficient, is characterized as changing things so that budget and recorded figures appear to match without requiring a change in either.

Chapter 2

Introduction to Zero-Base Budgeting

A HISTORICAL PERSPECTIVE

Before examining the general zero-base budgeting process, a brief historical review will provide a perspective for understanding its value for hospital financial managers. Some financial managers who are familiar with ZBB may believe, improperly, that the genesis was at Texas Instruments, Inc., or the state of Georgia.

The initial ZBB system was implemented in the Department of Agriculture in 1964 under the then secretary, Orville Freeman. A directive from his office to the department said:

> A new concept has been adopted ... namely, that of Zero-Base Budgeting. This means that all programs will be reviewed from the ground up and not merely in terms of changes proposed for the budget year ... The total work program of each agency must be subjected to an intensive review and evaluation ... Consideration must be given to the basic need for the work contemplated, the level at which the work should be carried out, the benefits to be received, and the costs to be incurred.
>
> The fact that certain activities have been carried out for a number of years will not, per se, adequately justify their continuation. Nor will the fact that programs are prescribed by statutory law necessarily be a controlling consideration. Program goals based on statutes enacted to meet problems or needs that are today of lesser priority must be reevaluated in terms of present conditions.
>
> It is implicit in the Zero-Based Budget approach that the need for programs and their recommended magnitude ... be clearly and specifically demonstrated ... The justification should be pre-

19

pared on the assumption that all information needed for making budget decisions should be included.

The implementation was unsuccessful for several reasons, among them:

- All agencies assumed their programs were necessary and prepared their budgets accordingly. There were few instances where budgets conformed with instructions.
- The timing acted as a constraint on the proper implementation of the new budget. The appropriation bill was behind schedule in Congress, and at that time the Billie Sol Estes scandal, with its accompanying impact on the department, had just developed.
- Those preparing the budgets were more concerned with the level of their appropriations than with whether they had need for the funds at all.
- The initial implementation created a considerable volume of paper work that was not managed properly.

Several benefits accrued from the department's experience, including an awareness by management of all elements entering the budget process and a greater participation by lower level managers in the budget's preparation.

In 1969, Arthur F. Burns, then chairman of the President's Council of Economic Advisers, said in a speech titled "The Control of Government Expenditures":

> Customarily, the officials in charge of an established program have to justify only the increase which they seek above last year's appropriation. In other words, what they are already spending is usually accepted as necessary, without examination. Substantial savings could undoubtedly be realized if [it were required that] every agency ... make a case for its entire appropriation request each year, just as if its program or programs were entirely new. Such budgeting procedure may be difficult to achieve, partly because it will be resisted by those who fear that their pet programs would be jeopardized by a system that subjects every ... activity to annual scrutiny of its costs and results.

The similarities between the Freeman directive and the Burns statement are unmistakable. Both refer to the nonjustification of existing programs and the necessity of presenting the entire budget request from nothing (or zero dollars) as if the requesting division were new. Perhaps just as importantly, both implied an evaluation of budget requests on a benefits/cost relationship, even though no methodology for measuring this illusive evaluation criterion was mentioned. Presumably programs with the greatest benefits relative to cost relationships would be funded before others.

The Texas Instruments Experience

In a 1970 issue of *Harvard Business Review*, Peter Pyhrr, then manager, staff control, at Texas Instruments, Inc. (TI) described ZBB as developed and used at his company in Dallas. The incident at Texas Instruments that prompted a move to ZBB is not uncommon and has occurred in health care institutions. TI had experienced increasing costs, but revenues were not keeping pace, so a budget cut was imminent. Cost center managers were asked to identify service reductions if the budget were reduced by 10 percent. Actual reductions would be 5 percent, chosen by top management from the 10 percent identified. This analysis showed, in detail, what would not be done if funding were decreased, but top management was not able to determine what was being done for the funding provided. A department-by-department investigation of the budget requests and their uses brought several problems to the surface:

- Some departments did not establish goals and objectives.
- Some of top management's goals could not be met with the amount of funding provided.
- Some decisions with alternative solutions, each requiring different cash flows, had not been included in the budget.
- Interdepartmental responsibilities and workloads were changed without corresponding shifts in budget allocations.

These problems prompted TI to seek a budget process that would help solve these problems. The result was ZBB. TI first used ZBB in 1970 for the staff and research divisions. Some of the benefits it found included:

1. More and better information was provided to top management for funding decisions.
2. Duplication of efforts were identified.
3. Priorities were identified within and among departments.
4. Activities and programs that could be added or deleted for budget increases or decreases were isolated.

State of Georgia Experience

After Jimmy Carter was elected governor of Georgia in 1970, he began reorganizing the state government's executive branch—a task that had been one of his central campaign planks. He was keenly interested in the work of Peter Pyhrr at Texas Instruments and the ZBB system in operation there. In 1971, Carter asked Pyhrr to serve as a consultant on implementation of a ZBB system in the Georgia government. This was to begin with the 1972–1973 fiscal year budget. Carter introduced his new ZBB concept in his "State of the State" address in January 1972. Later, in his Budget Address to the Joint Session of the General Assembly of Georgia, Carter said:

> Zero-base budgeting requires every agency in state government to identify each function it performs and the personnel and cost to the taxpayers for performing that function ....
> The intense analysis which goes into the construction of a decision package begins at a low level of management within an agency. Constant review and refinement take place at each succeeding level. Each agency assigns a priority to all of its decision packages, and this information is utilized in the allocation of funds in the budget ....
> By requiring department heads and their subordinates to take a close look at what they could do with *less* money, zero-base budgeting encourages the search for more efficient ways to do the job.
> By requiring clear descriptions of the results to be expected from every dollar spent, zero-base budgeting makes it possible to evaluate the performance of an agency against its budget ....
> As a result of these techniques we have a budget based on cost analysis and priority ranking. We have a budget in which justification for every dollar was required—for old programs as well as new.

Georgia found several advantages from using ZBB. The financial planning phase was shifted to prior to preparing the budget rather than concurrent with the budget preparation. ZBB enabled top management to receive better information on the functions of the government. State personnel became more involved in preparing the budget. These advantages did not occur without problems. One involves the increased time and effort for budget preparation. It was thought that with continued use and experience, the time would diminish.

The Federal Experience

In February 1977 President Carter requested each executive department and agency to develop a zero-base budget and to prepare the fiscal year

1979 budget using the system. Bert Lance, then director of the Office of Management and Budget, soon issued guidelines for a ZBB system for executive agencies. Carter's aim was to reduce federal waste, and implementation of ZBB was among his campaign promises. By early 1979, evidence on the success of ZBB still was sketchy, but the mere exercise of implementing the idea into the mammoth federal government left few who had been involved ambivalent toward it.

Experiences in the Private Sector

Numerous private companies have installed ZBB since Texas Instruments did so in 1970. A number have found significant benefits. Major U.S. corporations said ZBB was producing substantial savings. For example, the Southern California Edison Company reported savings of $300,000, the Ford Motor Company millions of dollars, and the Westinghouse Electric Company $4.2 million in overhead alone.

Traditional Incremental Budgeting vs. ZBB

Most budgeting systems that do not use ZBB involve a traditional incremental model. Incremental budgeting directs emphasis and attention toward the amounts added or subtracted from an existing budgetary base. Only the requests for additional funds are evaluated carefully before monies are committed. The base is assumed to be required and is accepted. The preparation of the budget under the incremental approach assumes that the average historical costs should be increased for an inflation factor, then new program costs added, to fix the upcoming year's budget figure. Justification is sought only for the new program costs.

ZBB, on the other hand, requires that the department heads break down their costs by levels of effort, programs, or functions. Each level and its funding then must stand the test of justification each year if it is to be retained. Any new programs and their estimated funding requirements will be evaluated along with the old. No assumed base of funding is used to add future allotments.

THE ZBB PROCESS

Establishment of Objectives

As an initial step before ZBB is made operational, department heads and managers establish objectives for each department or subunit in the hospital. The departmental objectives should be consistent with those established by the board and administration. Broad departmental objectives, such as providing quality health care at the lowest possible cost, are admirable; however, they are not specific enough to measure against results. Department objectives should be specific statements that include the anticipated or intended output for which the unit is designed. Examples of departmental objectives may include:

Housekeeping. Utilize present staff better so new hospital wing can be added to workload with no increase in FTEs.

Maintenance. Initiate staff training sessions in air-conditioning maintenance so minor repairs and maintenance of cooling and heating systems can be accomplished in-house.

Administration. Begin employee exercise program for men's and women's groups. Anticipate 30 percent of the staff will participate.

As objectives are being defined, department heads and management must determine performance criteria—input necessary for the output desired—against which results may be measured. Even if objectives are not defined and established firmly, ZBB may be implemented, although it will not achieve full effectiveness.

Preparation of Decision Packages

Basic to any ZBB system is the preparation and priority ranking of decision packages. A decision package is an incremental budget request that identifies and describes a specific activity and its required funding so management can evaluate its benefit and cost, rank it against other activities competing for available resources, and decide whether to approve or disapprove it. The format for a request should be such that each decision package can be compared in the department and with other decision packages in the organization. In a traditional budgeting system, participation by lower level management in the budget preparation process is desirable; when using ZBB, it is mandatory. Therefore, the decision package is prepared by the lowest level of management responsible for carrying out the objectives of a department (sometimes referred to as a decision unit).

Since the preparation of decision packages is so vital to the ZBB system, a department head must remember two considerations:

1. There may be more than one alternative to meeting the objectives of the decision unit.
2. There may be different levels of effort and funding needed to carry out the best alternative.

This means that a department head must establish alternatives, if feasible, then consider the effect of different levels of effort and funding on meeting the objectives of the decision package.

Each department head must establish a minimum level decision package for each decision unit. This package indicates the minimum funding necessary to retain the unit. The package also would indicate the output or contribution the function could make at that level of funding. For funding requests above the minimum, the department head must submit separate decision packages indicating the amount necessary and additional benefit. These decision packages generally have a common name and are numbered serially (1 of 3, 2 of 3, 3 of 3).

Exhibit 2-1 is an example of three separate decision packages submitted by the manager of patient accounts. The first decision package indicates the resources that will allow the patient billing function to operate at a minimum level. Only one clerk is necessary, but the time required to bill a patient is long. The department manager should indicate the effects of nonacceptance of the decision package and any alternative methods that may be used, such as contracting with an outside group to perform the function.

The second decision package should show the incremental cost as well as the total expense of meeting the current objective (last year's activity at current funding requirements). Justification for the incremental costs and the total of current level spending should accompany the decision package.

The third decision package and any further ones would present any additional costs of improving the current level of activity. Advantages or improvements should be described, as well as the effects of not accepting the package. The purpose for the process used in developing the packages is to make the manager think through different levels of funding for accomplishing the objectives while also giving upper management information it can use if funds are limited.

Ranking Decision Packages

The decision packages must be ranked by the department head in the order of their relative importance. Relative importance is governed by two criteria: (1) the contribution the package makes to the department's objectives, and (2) the amount of funding necessary for the package. Using these criteria, management can determine subjectively the effects of each package on the goals and objectives of the department and, simultaneously, the rankings can show the goals and objectives that may not be met if certain packages are omitted because of fund limitations.

After all the department heads have ranked their decision packages in

Exhibit 2-1 Decision Package—Minimum Activity Zero-Base Budget Request—1980*

DEPARTMENT: Patient Accounts
FUNCTION: Patient Billing

FUNCTIONAL ACTIVITY OBJECTIVES:
Provide a timely accumulation of patient charges and bill patient and third party payor, when applicable, in a minimum number of days after inpatient discharge or outpatient services.

MINIMUM DECISION PACKAGE: (1 of 3)
One (1) billing clerk necessary to bill patients within an average of twenty (20) working days from date inpatient is discharged or outpatient services are performed.

	FY79	FY80
Salaries (1 clerk)	$16,000	$8,500
Fringe benefits	1,600	850
Supplies	100	110
Total cost	17,700	9,460

EFFECTS OF NONACCEPTANCE:
Discontinue billing activity.

ALTERNATIVE METHODS OF PERFORMING SERVICE:
None available.

DEPARTMENT: Patient Accounts
FUNCTION: Patient Billing

FUNCTIONAL ACTIVITY OBJECTIVES:
Provide a timely accumulation of patient charges and bill patient and third party payor, when applicable, in a minimum number of days after inpatient discharge or outpatient services.

Source: Ray D. Dillon, "Zero-Base Budgeting: An Introduction." *Hospital Financial Management*, November–December 1977. Reprinted by permission of Hospital Financial Management Association, Chicago, Illinois.

Exhibit 2-1 Continued Decision Package—Current Objective Zero-Base
Budget Request—1980

CURRENT LEVEL FUNDING: (2 of 3)
Two (2) billing clerks necessary to bill patients within an average of
ten (10) working days from date outpatient services are performed or
inpatient is discharged.

	FY79	FY80	CUM*
Salaries (2 clerks)	$16,000	$8,500	$17,000
Fringe benefits	1,600	850	1,700
Supplies	100		110
Total cost	17,700	9,350	18,810

INCREASED WORKLOAD REQUIREMENTS:
None

EFFECTS OF NONACCEPTANCE:
Billing cycle will increase from ten to twenty days, adversely affecting
cash flow and patient relations.

DEPARTMENT: Patient Accounts
FUNCTION: Patient Billing

FUNCTIONAL ACTIVITY OBJECTIVES:
Provide a timely accumulation of patient charges and bill patient and
third party payor, when applicable, in a minimum number of days
after inpatient or outpatient services.

FUNDING REQUIRED ABOVE CURRENT LEVEL: (3 of 3)
One (1) additional billing clerk added to the present number of two
(2).

---

*Cumulative column is an addition of decision package requests for minimum activity and
current objective for FY 1980.

Exhibit 2-1 Continued Decision Package—Improvement Objective Level Zero-Base Budget Request—1980

	FY79	FY80	CUM*
Salaries (3 clerks)	$16,000	$8,500	$25,500
Fringe benefits	1,600	850	2,550
Supplies	100	50	160
Total Cost	17,700	9,400	28,210

DESCRIPTION OF ADDITIONAL SERVICES FOR FUNDING:
The advantage of the additional clerk will be a reduction in billing time from an average of ten working days to an average of five working days from inpatient release or outpatient services.

EFFECTS OF NONACCEPTANCE:
Billing cycle will remain at ten working days (see package 2 of 3). Cash flow will remain as it is, rather than increasing.

---

*Cumulative column is an addition of decision package requests for minimum activity, current objective, and improvement objective for FY 1980.

---

order of importance, management at the next highest level consolidates the rankings into a single ranking. Consolidation continues until the packages have reached the highest level of management, when a final single ranking prevails. It is from this that the budget is prepared.

The consolidating procedure becomes more difficult as the narrowness of expertise diminishes up through the management hierarchy. Department heads have a thorough knowledge of their specific objectives and goals and how they want to accomplish them. As upper management tries to merge the packages of several departments, judgment of the relative importance of proposals from different departments becomes increasingly difficult.

A possible solution to this problem is the use of a committee of department heads whose packages are being ranked, plus the manager who has the task of consolidation. During the committee's deliberations, the department heads can understand the goals and objectives of others and how their own department fits into the organizational big picture. This should lead ultimately to a ranking of packages that will prove the best in meeting the overall goals of the institution. The ranking procedure can be facilitated by adopting a standard form such as that in Exhibit 2-2. The sections of the form corresponding to the numbers in parentheses are as follows:

1. relative ranking of each decision package
2. name of package, with packages representing different levels of effort on funding for the same project shown as (1 of 4), (2 of 4), etc.
3. last year's budgeted amount for individual decision packages, including any amounts from grants or other sources outside the hospital
4. last year's budgeted amount for individual decision packages
5. full-time-equivalent personnel required for each decision package
6. funding for each decision package necessary this year from all sources
7. funding for each decision package necessary this year from hospital sources
8. full-time-equivalent personnel required this year for each decision package
9. cumulative total funding required this year from all sources
10. cumulative total funding required this year from hospital sources
11. cumulative total percentage of hospital funding for each decision package to total hospital funding for departments last year; this column provides the measure to compare to the cutoff point

During the ranking process, the department heads or managers should not be overly concerned about the relative rankings of decision packages that are meeting their objectives and goals and those of the hospital. They should be ranked high and funded. Packages representing new programs or additional effort or output for old programs may be ranked lower or higher than existing ones and should be reviewed carefully when deciding whether or not to include them. To assist managers during their review process, a cutoff point should be established so they will know which decision packages should receive a limited review and which a more rigorous appraisal. A possible approach to establishing a cutoff point would be to select an arbitrary percentage of the previous year's departmental budget. The percentage would be based on the number of packages the department has submitted. Generally, the more packages a department submits, the higher the arbitrary percentage cutoff point would be.

For example, assume that Department A submits 400 decision packages. In trying to appraise the rankings in that department, a manager would be faced with an insurmountable difficulty of deciding among the thousands of combinations, unless the cutoff point is high, say 80 percent. This means that the cumulative total dollar budget requests for the projects would be added until the total reached 80 percent of last year's departmental budget.

Exhibit 2-2 Decision Package Ranking Form

Rank (1)	Package Name (2)	Last Year's Budget			This Year's Budget			Cumulative Level		
		Total Funding (3)	Hospital Funding (4)	FTE (5)	Total Funding (6)	Hospital Funding (7)	FTE (8)	Total Funding (9)	Hospital Funding (10)	Cum. % (11)

Department: Prepared by: Date:

*Source: Ray D. Dillon, "Zero-Base Budgeting: An Introduction." *Hospital Financial Management*, November–December 1977. Reprinted by permission of Hospital Financial Management Association, Chicago, Illinois.

Decision packages that were included as a part of the 80 percent cutoff figure would receive a rather cursory review, while projects outside the 80 percent point would be reviewed carefully and ranked in order so that those that would provide the greatest contribution to organizational goals would be funded first. The process of ranking using a cutoff point is appropriate at all management levels.

Applicability of a ZBB System

A ZBB system can be applied to any department or function where a cost/benefit ratio of various decision packages must be determined subjectively. Furthermore, there often are revenue-generating centers that should be included in the ZBB system. During the early uses of zero-base budgeting, organizations focused their efforts primarily on service or supportive departments. Currently, greater interest is placed on revenue-generating departments, or profit centers. Often the only justification for additional funding required from the profit center was the revenue the requested money was expected to generate. A profit center supervisor never would be asked to justify any existing programs; therefore, existing resources could be used to support obsolete, ineffective, or marginally effective programs that were bringing in revenue just equal to the amount necessary for support. If profit center managers are required to prepare decision packages justifying each of their programs, they will be more inclined to determine carefully whether existing resources are being used effectively and resource requests are being funneled into the most appropriate functions.

In a hospital, service departments such as maintenance, housekeeping, administration, accounting, patient records, and others may find the ZBB process valuable. Clearly, a hospital may use both traditional budgeting and ZBB as complementary parts of its planning system. Traditional budgeting could be used in areas where the cost/benefit ratio may be expressed in dollars, while all other departments could apply ZBB.

Possible Advantages of a ZBB System

ZBB has the potential of reallocating funds to programs that provide the greatest benefit to the hospital. Funds can be shifted away from programs that produce little benefit and assigned to those that are providing or will provide greater benefit. By ranking the projects in order of their relative importance, management can determine better which are more important than others as it allocates limited funds. A ZBB system will provide a great amount of information to management that had not been available and that will help it direct the hospital more effectively. Finally, ZBB involves all levels of management in the budget preparation process. It also encourages them all to become thoroughly familiar with the activities under their control and the financial aspects related to those activities.

This last advantage also is a source of an implementation problem. This problem concerns (1) the great amount of time implementing the ZBB system takes during the first year, (2) the natural resistance by employees to the introduction of any new system, and (3) the resulting expense that will be incurred because of the time required.

SUMMARY

ZBB, as a concept, has been in existance for over 14 years. Its beginnings in the federal government almost went unnoticed. Only when Texas Instruments, Inc. adopted its use did the concept gain momentum. President Carter has further fostered its prominence as a management tool by introducing it to federal agencies for use in preparing the 1979 budget. Many corporations are adopting ZBB and report substantial cost savings because of it.

ZBB requires participation at all management levels in setting organizational objectives and in preparing the budget. Decision packages, key elements in the ZBB system, are incremental funding requests that indicate potential benefits to the organization if the packages are accepted. Prepared by the department manager, these packages are ranked in order of greatest organizational benefit. Succeeding higher level managers must consolidate the packages received from several departments until the highest level manager, president, or administrator has a consolidated listing of all packages prepared within the organization. The top administrative officer may then rerank packages for a final ranking and allocate funds to the departments based on the order of their package rankings.

The potential advantages of ZBB include: reallocating funds from the least to the most beneficial programs; providing information about present programs heretofore unavailable; and involving managers in budget preparation.

CONCLUSION

This overview of the zero-base budgeting model leaves unanswered many questions that will be resolved by detailing the procedures. The following chapters will study closely decision package design and formulation and the process of ranking the packages. The potential problems discussed briefly in this chapter will be examined in detail and solutions proposed. In the further analysis and discussion, it must be kept in mind that ZBB does not propose to make inefficient departments more efficient, nor does it transform inept department heads into able department managers. If used properly as a decision-making tool, it can provide management with an invaluable means of analysis and evaluation of present and future activities as a way to achieve the organization's goals and objectives.

To give the reader a better insight into the use of zero-base budgeting, the following three articles are included. The first, "Steps to Success with Zero-Base Budgeting Systems," reports the installation and use of a zero-base budgeting system in a municipality. Terrell Blodgett, a principal with the public accounting firm of Peat, Marwick, Mitchell & Co., emphasizes what he calls the 17 steps to success when implementing zero-base budgeting. The second article, "Zero-Base Budgeting: How To Get Rid of Corporate Crabgrass," is a report by Donald N. Anderson, former budget director for the Southern California Edison Company, on that organization's experience with zero-base budgeting. Included in the article are forms the company used for its decision packages and ranking the packages. The final article, "Zero-Base Budgeting: A Comparison With Traditional Budgeting," is by two professors of accountancy, Harper A. Roehm and Joseph F. Castellano of Wright State University, Fairborn, Ohio. This reviews both incremental and zero-base budgeting systems, with particular attention on the behavioral difficulties that may be encountered when using the zero-base system.

Readings

STEPS TO SUCCESS WITH ZERO-BASE BUDGETING SYSTEMS*

This widely heralded management method holds great promise for controlling costs in cities, large and small. The author, an experienced city manager, explains how the system works and then suggests how it can best be implemented.

Professional judgments about zero-base budgeting (ZBB) cover the whole gamut between boundless enthusiasm and utter mistrust. President Carter ordered federal government agencies to prepare their next budgets in accordance with this technique, following the lead of at least eleven state governments and half a dozen cities. His decision was generally applauded as the solution to "budget creep," which has been putting government at all levels in increasingly difficult financial positions.

Yet many authorities on government management have serious doubts about ZBB. One respected professor, writing in *The Wall Street Journal*, went so far as to label it a "fraud." Concerned citizens may well wonder whether ZBB will prove to be a financial wonder drug or just snake oil.

This article will attempt to explain the workings of ZBB for government organizations, especially municipalities. It will evaluate its benefits and shortcomings. The major emphasis, however, will be placed on how to get ZBB started on the right track. For ZBB, like other management methods, can be either an extremely useful control or just another way to appear more efficient.

---

*Reprinted from *Management Controls* by Terrell Blodgett by permission of Peat, Marwick, Mitchell & Co., © November–December, 1977.

Why Introduce ZBB?

ZBB was formally delineated and put into practice for the first time by Texas Instruments, Inc., just fifteen years ago.* Since then it has been adopted by several other noteworthy companies, including Xerox, Allied Van Lines, and Westinghouse Electric. Their objective has been to allocate resources more rationally and efficiently.

The majority of cities and states adopting ZBB (mainly in the last few years) have had a similar purpose. Most have acted under orders from elected governing bodies, such as city councils or legislatures, which have been motivated partly by a desire to convince their constituents that they are doing something to curb the rising costs of government.

Alternatively, the new budgetary technique may be launched by the chief executive. Reasons advanced by administrators for the changeover include:

- The incremental nature of the existing budget process, in which department heads generally consider existing programs already justified and thus justify only the "new money" they ask for.
- The executive probably wants more information to be developed for the budget process regarding the services of the city—their nature, the level, the beneficiaries, and the required resources.
- He may very well want the information in the current budget process to be "packaged" so that decisions of reduced or increased funding can be made in a logical, informed manner and the impact of more or less money can be predicted.
- And he wants to engage supervisors and foremen below the department head level in the budget process. This emphasizes budget accountability at the subdepartment level and furthers these supervisors' professional development generally.

ZBB Is a Map of Rational Change

The person generally credited with first using the term "zero-base budgeting" publicly is Arthur Burns, Chairman of the Federal Reserve Board. In 1969 he told a meeting of the Tax Foundation that "a reform of vital significance [to the control of government expenditures] would be the adoption of zero-base budgeting." Burns knew first-hand that most government agencies, at the federal, state, or local level, assumed that whatever

---

Note: According to published sources Texas Instruments, Inc. first used ZBB in 1969— *eight* years prior to Mr. Blodgett's article.

they were currently spending was accepted as necessary and all they had to justify in each budget were the increases above the previous year's appropriation. He believed it would be healthy for every agency to make a fresh case for its entire appropriation each year.

Thus the concept of zero-base budgeting—at least theoretically—is that managers of an activity have to justify *everything* they want to do in the new budget year. Rather than merely modifying the previous year's budget or justifying only the increases, managers must start afresh. They must develop the rationale and determine the resources required for alternative levels of service. Accordingly, all programs, new or old, and the various levels of service, are given equal opportunity to find their places in the final budget.

There are four key steps in the ZBB process:

1. The definition of "decision units," sometimes called "basic budgetary units."
2. The analysis of decision units to decide the appropriate alternative service levels and the preparation of "decision packages" to describe those various levels of service.
3. The "ranking" of the decision packages in order of priority, first by the persons directly responsible for the programs and then up through the chain of command until there is a citywide ranking, determined largely by the people having responsibility for the entire municipality.
4. The presentation of the budget to the governing body.

Decision Units and How They Are Chosen

A decision unit, the basic ingredient of ZBB, is usually defined as a basic activity or group of activities that management considers for planning, analysis, and review. In other words, a decision unit is generally the lowest level for which budget decisions are made. In municipalities, each decision unit is normally an organizational unit, although it can also be a program, a project, a line item, or a capital project.

The selection of a decision unit is a critical step. Choosing organizational units with multiple activities and large budgets can defeat the objective of sorting out individual programs that ought to be eliminated if made to stand scrutiny by themselves. On the other hand, a decision unit that consists of too small an activity can require analysis and paperwork out of proportion to possible benefits.

ZBB has no absolute dictums, definitions, or procedures, and the selection of the decision unit is no exception. Considerations such as the size of the organization, its range of activities, and the availability of accounting and workload data should dictate the size and extent of the decision unit. In one city, for example, accounting information was available down to the section level in large departments and to the division level in smaller departments. This city chose these levels as their decision units and worked with the resulting 125 units.

Decision Packages

The first step at setting budget levels: Once the decision units are selected, each decision-unit manager is asked to analyze his activity and to consider various service levels. One might be a minimal level that can operate with appreciably smaller funds than are allocated in the current budget. Another level might be an intermediate level requiring approximately the same funds as the current level. And, finally, additional levels above the current level are worth considering.

While the name of the system is zero-base budgeting, the unit managers do not have to submit a "zero package." The essential services, e.g., fire and police protection or refuse collection and disposal, must be provided and require some level of funding. The question is at what level the service should be provided and how much funding this requires.

For each service level, the manager prepares an analysis and presents it in a "decision package," which is the aggregate of his service level's analyses. Each package generally contains a statement of the objectives for the decision unit, a description of its activities, definitions, and statistics for work-load performance, personnel and cost requirements, funding sources, alternative methods for performing the decision unit's activities, and the consequences of *not* funding the package. The description of a decision package can run from one to three pages, depending on the detail of information desired.

A minimum of three decision packages is usually prepared for each decision unit. The maximum is generally four to five, although some imaginative and eager unit managers have submitted as many as ten packages for a single decision unit.

Setting Budget Priorities

The next step is ranking the decision packages from related decision units. The ranking represents an opinion as to which level of service should get funded first, which level second, and so on. It is done by the person responsible for the different decision units, who places relative values on the decision packages submitted by the heads of the units. As he does his ranking, he prepares a "ranking sheet," which lists the packages in priority order, specifies the cost and personnel required by each package, and also specifies the cumulative cost at each level in the ranking.

For example, a manager may be in charge of three decision units. If decision unit "A" prepares three packages, decision unit "B" four packages, and decision unit "C" three packages, the manager will have ten decision packages to rank in priority order.

The manager then submits his ranking sheet to his superior who evaluates the recommendations for funding decision packages in conjunction with recommendations made by the other managers at the same level. In other words, the superior develops an overall ranking for his entire area of responsibility. He is not bound to the relative rankings assigned by his subordinates but has a free hand to rank the packages in his area as he sees fit.

Ranking continues all the way up to the chief executive, who does it for the entire budget. He might assume this responsibility personally, delegate it to a committee of top assistants or department heads, or have the budget office make preliminary judgments, which he then would review in consultation with department heads.

One of the criticisms leveled at ZBB is that the high-level managers generally have no objective or measurable criteria with which to rank the packages presented to them. This has been true in many organizations. Although it is desirable to have a clearly delineated set of goals and objectives for each of the organization's functions and units and to have some objective ranking criteria, the fact is that ranking at this point may need to take place as it has always been done—by the subjective judgment of the division and department heads on what they perceive to be the objectives, priorities, and needs of the unit and the city.

Once the decisions are made on the inclusion of packages, the detailed budget is compiled for presentation to the city council. ZBB does not require major changes in budget format, but it does provide substantially more and clearer information. For example, the major policy decisions can be identified in the front of the budget document; then the manner in which each decision package supports one or more policy decisions can be set forth in the package. Hence, the decision makers have information that helps them make more logical decisions.

Starting the Organization's First ZBB

The ZBB concept is not complex or esoteric. Indeed, it is an extremely logical approach to arriving at a budget that provides the essential services,

Exhibit 2-3 The New Look in Budgeting

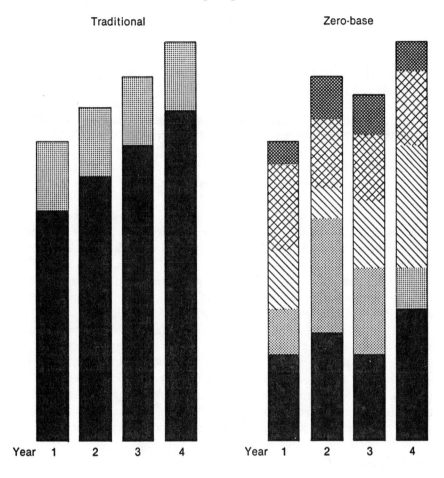

All too commonly, annual budgets for all or part of an organization are based mainly on the previous year's budget. As shown above, the budget for year one is accepted as a "given"; then a percentage is added for cost-of-living increases, inflation, and other contingencies to arrive at the budget for year two. Such creeping growth tends to be repeated almost indefinitely. Zero-base budgeting, in theory and often in practice, compels the budget makers to start afresh each year by breaking the total into components that are clearly visible and can be rated according to their importance. Each year, the bottom block represents a bare-bones amount (usually not zero). Upon this are stacked less important blocks, the upper ones representing what the organization might spend if money were no object. Then budget makers can decide where to draw the cutoff line. This may be higher or lower than the previous year's budget total, but at least it reflects a considered balancing of what is needed against what funds may be available.

yet ensures that an organization is staying within its means. What is difficult
and requires special attention is the implementation process. A government
should follow a complete and carefully defined implementation plan. The
most significant requisites are:

- a clearly stated set of goals and objectives for the organization as a
  whole and for each of the component units;
- a well-structured set of criteria for workload measurement;
- an accounting system capable of generating financial and budgetary
  data for the city's organizational units and program efforts; and
- a professional budget staff to guide the ZBB efforts and coordinate
  the entire changeover in the budget process, plus the ability to augment
  this staff with outside assistance if necessary.

Few municipalities can enjoy the luxury of having all four requisites
operational before the request comes from the city council: "We want next
year's budget prepared by ZBB techniques and procedures." Accounting
data available at the decision unit level is vital. If the city's accounting
system identifies costs only to the department head level, for example, and
the city desires to define decision units at a lower level, problems will
arise in arriving at defensible costs for the lower-level units.

Next, there must be at least one adequately trained budget person who
will guide and coordinate the entire ZBB effort. This person must take the
lead in setting the timetable for completion of the various steps, preparing
and training the department heads and supervisors in the entire ZBB
process, rendering technical assistance to the departments in the actual
preparation of their decision packages, checking the package submissions
as they are submitted, and assisting in the city-wide ranking process.

Seventeen Steps to Success

Experience shows that the following steps provide a simple, effective
process for the city that has decided to implement ZBB:

1. Fix responsibilities: Any project of the magnitude of ZBB requires
the fixing of responsibilities for the various steps among all concerned
individuals and groups, e.g., the city council, the chief executive, department, division, and section heads, budget staff, and outside consultants if
employed. More specifically, the responsibility for preparation of a budget
calendar should probably be assigned to the budget staff, and the responsibility for approval of that calendar should be assumed by the chief executive
or the city council. These responsibilities should be fixed at the beginning

of the process, defined in writing, and then adhered to during the budget preparation.

2. Develop a budget calendar: The responsible person or group, i.e., budget staff or project team—should prepare a budget calendar. With a normal, on-going budget process, the calendar might begin as late as six months prior to the beginning of the fiscal year. For the first year under ZBB, however, more time will be required. The budget process, rather than starting during the seventh month of the fiscal year, needs to be initiated in the third or fourth month of the year. This schedule would provide department heads and other responsible officials additional time to become familiar with the ZBB process and to prepare competent decision packages. Other reasons for starting earlier is that time will be required for ranking and the chief executive may well want to allow more time for the governing body's consideration of the recommended budget.

The earlier starting date will not always be necessary. In subsequent years, the city should be able to shorten the budget process and match the starting date of its former budget process.

3. Define certain policies and procedures: Before departments are able to prepare their decision packages, several preliminary questions must be answered at the citywide level. Should the ZBB include all of the city's funds? Most cities prepare basic budgets covering only their so-called general funds. Many operations, e.g., utilities, library, and perhaps others, as well as operations financed by federal or other outside funds are not included in the general fund. At what spending levels should the units be submitting packages? This is usually stated in percentages of current expenditures, e.g., 50 percent, 75 percent, 90 percent, 100 percent. Usually, the decision is made by first defining the minimum level. This minimum level then generally determines the appropriate levels for the second, third, and subsequent packages. The decision should obviously consider the economic condition during the budget year. The tighter the situation, the lower the levels should be set. Growing cities, however, might consider mandating the minimum-level package "not to exceed 90 percent of current expenditures."

What ZBB forms are to be used? During the first year, cities will probably want to use a three-to-four-page decision package form. Much can then be reduced in complexity and length in subsequent years: e.g., budgetary and accounting decisions regarding such matters as level of expense detail to be required in the decision packages; the procedure for handling capital-project items; the approach to handling salary increases; methods for recognizing nondepartmental items, such as utility costs and insurance; and minimum and maximum dollar size of packages. All of

Exhibit 2-4 Use of ZBB Techniques in Budget Formulation

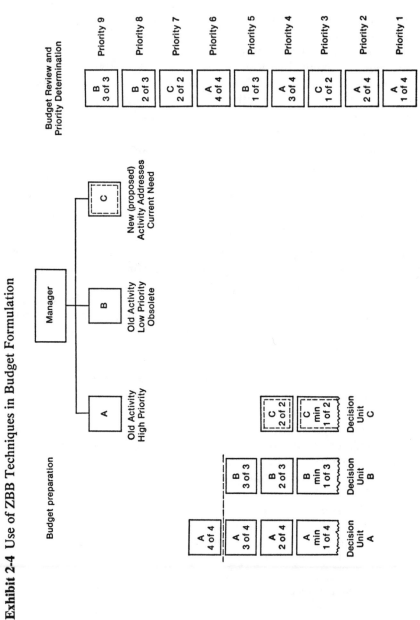

Exhibit 2-5 Early Phase of a Hypothetical Department's Decision Process

Summary assessment of community services

Importance	Stage of development				
	Most inadequate	More inadequate than most	Average adequacy	More adequate than most	Most adequate
Most important	Low-income housing (G) Group day care (S)				
More important	Homemaking (S)	Financial assistance (G) Hospital care-chronic (G) Hospital care-mental (G) Nursing home care (S) Sheltering aged (S) Visiting nurse svcs (S)	Environ-sanitation (G) Family counseling (G) Mental diagnosis (S)	Hospital care-acute (S) Medical diagnosis (S)	
Average importance		Casefinding (S) Detention-delinquents (G) Foster family care (S) Legal counseling (S)	Dental care (S) Detention-adults (G) Individual counseling (P) Protective services (G) Rehabilitation svcs (S) Sheltering-children (S) Sheltering-retarded (G) Social rehabilitation (P) Vocational counseling (S)	Adoption (P) Character building (P) Disease control (G) Health education (S) Informal education (P)	
Less important		Sheltered work (S)	Family life education (S) Friendly visiting (P) Residential GRP care (P) Sheltering-homeless (S) Sheltering-unwed (G) Short-term counseling (S) Transportation (P)	Camping (P) Disaster relief (S) Physical education (S)	
Least important			Transient accommodations (S)		Social recreation (S)

Financial responsibility codes: G—Mostly government; P—Mostly private; S-Shared government and private these decisions should be incorporated into a budget manual to be distributed to department heads and other key officials at the orientation session (which is discussed subsequently).

4. Consider a pilot-project approach: The city should consider whether it wants to adopt ZBB by having just a few departments install the system in the first year on a pilot-project basis. There are arguments pro and con. The advantages of the pilot-project approach are that the effort prepares the way for the remaining departments. It also enables a city to work out the "bugs" so that full implementation can proceed in a more orderly fashion. The disadvantages are that most city departments do not relish the idea of serving as a guinea pig, that no practical advantage is gained by segregating one or two departments from the rest, and that no ranking of packages can be accomplished with a pilot, since there is no citywide mechanism to be ranked against. Further, a pilot-project approach can be used in an attempt to satisfy an elected official with a "we gave it a try and, see, it didn't work" response.

5. Conduct an orientation seminar: Training of departmental personnel is another important preliminary step. It should start with an orientation seminar for department heads. This can be a two-hour department meeting to present the history, concepts, principles, and terminology of ZBB to stress the value of departmental goals, objectives, and work-load measures.

The opening seminars can also be used to describe where ZBB is now being used and the benefits that have resulted. Indeed, reading material describing the experiences of other cities and organizations should be given to the officials in order that they may learn about the experiences of others. Finally, it is a good idea to ask the department heads to take time following the seminar to consider and then establish or reconfirm their department's goals, objectives, and work-load measures.

6. Define decision units: At this point the city is ready to define its decision units. To accomplish this critical task, we suggest a joint approach. The department heads should define their decision units following instructions from the budget staff. The budget staff should then review and suggest changes. The end result should be a reasonable number of decision units that reflect the way the city is organized to provide services.

7. Conduct training workshops for personnel who will be preparing the budget: The next step is to train people for their role in formulation of decision units and packages and ranking. This training should be provided for all management, including the lower-level supervisors. One of the strengths of ZBB is the involvement of personnel who are at the operating level, but who have not taken part previously in budget preparation.

The training workshop should be approximately four to six hours. The principles of ZBB should be discussed, but this should be followed by specific exercises in working with ZBB decision packages in order to give the participants a "hands on" feeling for their tasks. The workshop should also provide instructions for the completion of every block on the ZBB forms. In contrast to the orientation seminar, which is more general, the purpose of the training workshops is to impart specific information in order that the departmental officials can return to their departments and begin preparation of the ZBB packages.

8. Prepare decision packages: Following the training session, departmental managers should be given reasonable time to consider how the functions for which they are responsible serve the community, to decide how these services can be provided in the ensuing year, and to develop their decision packages. These instructions should be part of a budget manual containing illustrative completed forms. During this time, the budget staff should visit the departments to render technical assistance in the new procedures.

9. Rank decision packages in the department: The next step is for each department to rank its decision packages. In small cities the work would be done entirely by the department head. In larger cities with divisions and sections below the department level, the division heads will first rank all of their sections; the department head will then take the divisional rankings and combine them into an overall departmental ranking for all divisions and sections in the department.

10. Review of decision packages by budget staff: At this point the department heads submit to the budget office all of the packages prepared by their personnel plus their own ranking sheet. The submissions should be on a staggered basis with smaller departments having earlier deadlines than the larger departments. The first step for the budget staff is to review the packages for completeness and adherence to the instructions. This can be facilitated by using a decision package check sheet that lists each block in the ZBB form and specifies the kind of response that should be in each block. Also, since a computer is often used in the budget preparation process, photocopies of the decision package forms can be sent to the data processing center, and the computer used to check the arithmetic calculations.

11. Analysis of decision packages by budget staff: The next step for the budget staff is analysis of the submissions. While the decision packages and departmental ranking sheets can go directly to the chief executive of his designated group for a citywide ranking, it is advisable to have the budget staff first review each package. They should be alert to certain recurring problems:

- Departmental personnel may attempt "gamesmanship"—e.g., by ranking packages out of order. Packages that are obvious necessities are ranked low with the thought in mind that they will have to be funded even if they miss the cutoff line.
- The packages may include too small or too large dollar amounts for useful analysis. These can usually be detected by identifying more than one level of service that has been compressed into a single package.
- There may be obvious discrepancies in expenditure or work-load estimates that do not correspond to personnel estimates to accomplish the same level of service.

12. Estimate revenues for the new year: During the time the department heads and budget staff are preparing and analyzing the decision packages, another individual should be making revenue estimates for the new year. Preliminary estimates can be made early to give general guidance to the preparation of decision packages, i.e., the percentages of the current year's spending at which to develop the packages. As the year moves on, the revenue estimates for the new year should be sharpened so that by the time the departmental rankings and reviews are completed, the budget staff is able to submit a fairly accurate estimate of next year's revenues.

13. City-wide ranking of decision packages: The task of ranking all decision packages across the complete spectrum of a city has probably brought as much criticism to ZBB as any other single step. No doubt it is difficult for a single chief executive or even a team to rank all the packages, particularly if there are several thousand.

The first consideration, therefore, is to minimize the complexity right from the start by setting an arbitrary limit on the number of packages. The next suggestion is not to be afraid to innovate when doing the city-wide ranking.

14. Hold a training session for the governing body: The chief executive should conduct a briefing session with whatever legislative body is going to review the budget prior to its submission. The purpose is to acquaint the members with the new process that was used to develop the budget they will be receiving, to explain what the document will look like and how they can benefit from this format, and otherwise to set the stage for their consideration of the budget document. If the council initiated the entire process, it would be well also to have a session with the group at the beginning of the process.

15. Submit budget to the governing body: At this point the chief executive submits his budget to the governing body. It is built from the citywide rankings of expenditure requests and the revenue estimates. The chief executive might consider supplementing this basic recommendation with some of the documentation used to develop the budget. It would provide a foundation in case the governing body wanted to hold hearings with departments.

16. Review and adoption of the budget by the governing body: The role of the governing body in the budget process should be planned from the beginning. If its expectations have been properly considered and met, the review and adoption of the budget by the governing body should go quite smoothly.

17. Subsequent years: ZBB is still new and there is no logic that requires a city to follow the first year's procedures precisely in subsequent years. Indeed, the first city to adopt ZBB is now in its fourth year and has changed its emphasis each year. Thus, after the first year, the city's budget staff should evaluate the process and adopt modifications for improvement.

For instance, forms can generally be simplified. Analytical effort can be concentrated on internal administrative services and policies affecting the entire organization, such as wage and salary programs, data processing, telephone costs, or vehicle management, or on one functional area, e.g., the public-works area, which may seem to merit attention. Still another approach is to place emphasis on other methods of performing the service in question. This is rarely addressed adequately in the first year or two, even though it deserves substantial attention.

Practical Advice for Starting ZBB

Cities that have tried ZBB are beginning to learn much from their brief experiences. In conclusion, here is a list of the most important lessons in the form of practical advice:

- Anticipate what the council wants and expects from ZBB. It may be nothing more than a slightly altered budget format, or it may be much more. If the expectations are not foreseen and planned for, a bad experience can result.
- Anticipate a possibly negative reaction from the chief executive. Where the governing body has initiated ZBB, the chief executive may not be entirely friendly to the process. The executive's attitude can greatly influence success or failure.

- Build on the existing budget process and forms where possible. ZBB requires enough changes in forms, procedures, and habits. Try to utilize existing procedures and forms wherever possible.
- Define decision units carefully. This simple early step is vitally important. Time spent in a thorough analysis of what level of the organization should be utilized for decision units will be more than recouped later.
- Question the workload statistics presented. Few departments in few cities have developed their work-load statistics to a high degree of accuracy. The budget staff should question these statistics carefully and critically and provide technical assistance to the departments in improving the reliability of the information.
- Anticipate the volume of decision packages and prepare alternative approaches to handle it.
- Decide how salary increases will be budgeted. If the decision at the beginning of the process is to eliminate all salary increases, i.e., cost-of-living and merit, from initial package figures, then there should be a way at the time of citywide rankings to insert salary considerations. If they are not inserted and the chief executive makes his priority listing without regard to salary increases, he is telling the council that to increase salaries, taxes must be increased.
- One way to handle salary increases is to have four to six packages prepared that are "salary packages" only. These could be packages based on the costs of 3 percent, 5 percent, and 7 percent cost-of-living increases, and packages setting aside amounts for merit increases.
- Provide space on the decision package forms for federal and supplemental funding. One of the advantages of ZBB cited by virtually every city using it has been the additional information on supplemental funding available to the decision unit. As a result, many governing bodies are requesting chief executives to bring decision making on all budgets—the general fund budget, the general revenue-sharing budget, and the community development budget—into one time frame so that the total needs of the city may be considered and budgeted together.
- Don't be overly concerned the first year with lack of information on alternative methods for providing a service. The block entitled "Alternative methods of providing this service" has uniformly been completed in the poorest, most incomplete fashion. This is a vitally important part of the ZBB process, but can wait until subsequent years for concerted effort.
- Manage the paperwork and remember to emphasize "substance over form." Perhaps the most frequent criticism of ZBB is the amount of

time and paper it requires. There is no question it requires more of both the first year, although the time element decreases in subsequent years.

The essential idea is to concentrate on the quality of information gathered, not the quantity. And as ZBB grows from infancy to maturity, its true value will be judged by the extent to which it improves the quality of government.

ZERO-BASE BUDGETING: HOW TO GET RID OF
CORPORATE CRABGRASS*

by Donald N. Anderson

Instead of using current budgets as a starting point for next year's operations, many companies now start from ground zero in each year's budgeting process. This approach forces managers to assess their operations from the ground up and justify every dollar spent in terms of overall corporate goals.

For companies in a budget squeeze, the obvious target for quick remedial action is that portion of the income statement most amenable to management control—controllable operation and maintenance expenses. But exercises in crash budget reductions too often yield only temporary improvements.

During the past two or three years, rising operating costs and declining growth rates have put companies in a profitability crunch that demands significant, innovative approaches to doing something about improving bottom-line results. And managers who have had to make agonizing decisions on budgets now realize that for favorable long-term results, you need budgetary reductions that will stick.

Administering operating budgets, however, is a lot like getting crabgrass out of your lawn. You can apply weed killers to eradicate it or pull it out by the roots, but despite expensive chemicals and backbreaking work, crabgrass usually creeps back—and the weekend gardener's job is never really done.

The parallel between "managing" crabgrass and administering a corporate budget is not so far fetched as it might seem. Corporations and their managers have crabgrass activities in their budgets that compete for the same dollars needed by essential, basic activities. We can mow budgets and take 5 to 10 percent off the top, but that doesn't affect the crabgrass. We can selectively pull out crabgrass activities, but if we don't get the roots out, it isn't long before people and dollars are drawn into the same activities again. What's needed is a kind of selective treatment that can be applied to the entire budget to knock out the weeds and provide an overall net reduction—while keeping the desired activities functioning efficiently.

A technique that many companies are adapting and implementing to improve their budgetary front lawns is called Zero-Based Operational Planning and Budgeting (ZBOP). It's a formula we use at Southern California Edison, and we believe it does a good job of getting rid of budgetary crabgrass and keeping it out.

Improving on Traditional Techniques

Although the buzz words "zero-base budgeting" are relatively new to many managers, the underlying concept is nothing more than a systemization of traditional operational planning and budgeting processes. In recent years, however, the traditional processes have not measured up to the tough decision making required because they assume that the projects and ongoing activities making up the historical budget base are (1) essential to the mission of the company and must be continued during the budget year; (2) are being performed in an optimal, cost-efficient manner; and (3) are projected to be cost-effective in the budget year, requiring budget dollar increases only for uncontrollables such as pay increases and materials costs.

Some projects and activities do, of course, meet these criteria, but it is unrealistic to assume that all do. It becomes a question, then, of which activities and projects are not really essential and what criteria should be used for making a judgment. The answers must come from a joint effort of each manager, his boss, and the members of senior management. This combination—which ensures that both corporate and individual organization needs are satisfied—is the essence of the ZBOP approach.

How ZBOP Works

The zero-base approach has two fundamental steps. The first requires preparation of a decision-oriented summary plan for each activity or project. Called a "decision package," this summary (operational plan) usually includes a statement of the expected business result or purpose of the activity, its costs, personnel required, measures of performance, alternative courses of action, and an evaluation—from a corporate or organizationwide perspective—of the *benefits of performance and consequences of nonperformance.* In developing the summary plan, each manager must evaluate two types of alternatives:

- Different ways of performing each activity (for example, in-house versus contracted maintenance services), and
- Different levels of effort and resources required for performing each activity.

Managers also must identify a minimum level of spending for each activity and then identify in separate decision packages the costs and benefits of incremental, additional levels of spending.

The second fundamental step in ZBOP requires that each decision package be ranked against packages for other current and proposed new activities and projects, thus allowing each manager to specify his priorities for new and old programs. The end result is a prioritized list of priced-out operational plans built from the ground up, or "zero base."

The list can be used by senior management to evaluate and compare relative needs and priorities in making crucial funding decisions. As the list of approved operational plans increases, the total cost also increases, and top management can decide at what point the added costs outweigh the benefits.

Under this procedure, the entire budgeting process need not be recycled back through the operating organizations when expenditure levels must be changed; instead, the decision-package ranking identifies the activities, projects, and operations (as summarized in the decision packages) to be added or deleted to implement a budget change. As an additional benefit, managers at all organizational levels become involved in the process, and they develop a greater sense of responsibility for budgets and related accomplishments. The zero-base documents provide a convenient reference plan that they can use for controlling their activities during the operating year.

Getting Started in ZBOP

The prospect that 1974 earnings would fail to meet company objectives prompted Southern California Edison to begin experimenting with the ZBOP concept. The need for prompt, effective action of some kind had been foreseen in December 1973 during the wrapup of the 1974 budgeting process when fuel shortages, rising prices, and reduced sales resulting from a statewide energy conservation program pointed to projected earnings substantially below 1974 goals. As a result, department managers were directed to submit by mid-January 1974 their estimates of activities that could be reduced and the expected consequences of such action.

During an all-day meeting of the SCE Management Committee held early in February, each manager was given an opportunity to explain and defend his proposed budget revisions. The session, which provided senior managers with broad visibility over the operational aspects of the proposed budget changes, was the first time senior managers had an opportunity to participate actively in budgeting and concurrent activity-planning decisions on a companywide basis.

Subsequent discussions of senior managers focused on development of a stategy to be used in preparing budgets for 1975. The arbitrariness of "crash" reductions by either specifying a spending limit, as was done for the 1974 budget, or ordering an across-the-board percentage cut, was acknowledged. Rapid changes occurring in the 1974 business environment, however, made it clear that the planning and budgeting processes had to be made more flexible and responsive to unanticipated changes in costs, revenues, and operating conditions. The idea of developing contingency plans for each of a series of alternative assumptions concerning 1975 business conditions was tested briefly and discarded for two reasons: excessive paperwork would be required, and development of contingency plans to meet hypothetical future conditions is a concept that does not appeal to busy, pragmatic operating managers.

At this point, it became apparent that a zero-base planning and budgeting approach might be useful to Southern California Edison, and the Management Committee agreed to (1) a pilot test of the entire zero-base process in six small staff departments reporting to the financial vice-president and (2) the use of portions of the process in all other departments.

The results of the 1974 pilot test were, of course, limited, but over all, it was an enlightening learning experience. Some of its benefits and lessons were:

- The budget director's staff had an opportunity to begin counseling departments concerning the benefits of analytical operational planning aimed at achieving long-term cost savings through changes in operation, organization, work processes, and so forth, as opposed to remedial actions having only a short-run effect in improving earnings. Managers thus were encouraged to weigh alternatives and evaluate them in terms of the dollar consequences to the company as a whole even though some alternatives might require the addition of personnel to the company payroll. Evaluation of benefits from a companywide perspective also was encouraged.
- We found that budgeting activity in the company was viewed by many as a numbers-oriented clerical exercise that managers frequently delegated to staff personnel; also there was a continuing attitude that the burden of proof as to where and how much a proposed budget should be reduced rested with the budget staff (and the Management Committee).
- This inappropriate over-concern with the clerical aspects of filling in numbers on forms pointed to an apparent need for budgeting guidelines emphasizing the crucial managerial aspects of the process. Logically, the burden of justifying all components of a proposed bud-

get rests with the responsible operating manager because he is in the best position to know where and how much budgets can be reduced without seriously jeopardizing the company.

Exhibit 2-6 Highlights of the ZBOP Process

1. Under the traditional budgeting technique, you:

   • Fit a trend line to historical recorded data and extrapolate to the budget year.
   • Assume that the current "base" is made up of only necessary cost-efficient activities that should be perpetuated.
   • Concentrate on justifying the incremental increase only.

   In the chart below each block represents dollars needed to perform a project or continuing assignment having a defined scope of work and time schedule.

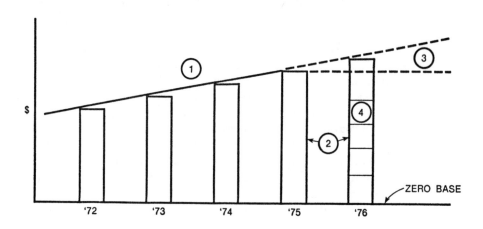

2. In ZBOP, each project and each continuing work activity must be broken down into smaller elements for detailed analysis and planning (see chart *below*). To avoid excessive detail, however, an element should comprise no less than one full person and all associated costs.

If the element involves no employees (as in the case of contracted work), the dollar value should generally not be less than some meaningful minimum, say $10,000.

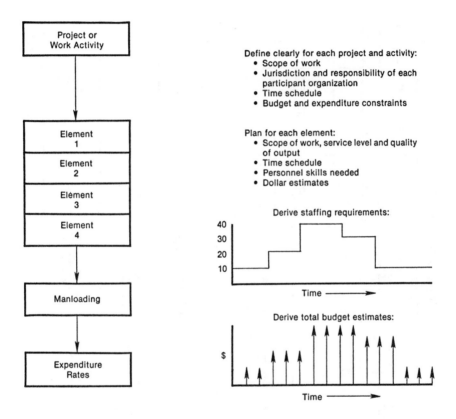

3. Analysis summaries—"decision packages"—for each level of effort are then prepared. A sample decision-package form is illustrated in the next example. A fundamental step in the ZBOP process, the form summarizes a scope of work, cost, personnel, and implied time schedule, plus assessments of the benefits of performing the work and the expected consequences if it is not. The format makes it relatively easy for a manager to decide whether or not the work should be done and what its relative priority is.

DECISION PACKAGE

Objective No. _____

ACTIVITY (OR OBJECTIVE) NAME	DEPARTMENT			PREPARED		RANK
PBX MAINTENANCE AND SUBSET INSTALLATIONS	COMMUNICATIONS			RALPH SCHWARTZ		5
	DIVISION			APPROVED		
LEVEL NO. 2 OF 3	CENTRAL			B. MILLER		
				Date August 15, 1975		

	RESOURCES REQUIRED*	CURRENT YEAR (75)	BUDGET YEAR (76)
	Personnel	2	2
	Labor $	28	30
	Outside Services $	0	0
	Other $	2	2
	Total $	30	32

PURPOSE OF ACTIVITY

MAINTAIN COMPANY-OWNED PBX TELEPHONE SWITCHING EQUIPMENT AND RELATED EQUIPMENT TO PROVIDE RELIABLE INTRA-COMPANY COMMUNICATIONS AND DEPENDABLE LINKAGES WITH THE BELL SYSTEM NETWORK.

DESCRIPTION OF ACTIVITY

THIS LEVEL PROVIDES SUPERVISORS FOR BOTH THE DAY AND SWING SHIFTS. THIS LEVEL PLUS 1 OF 3 COMPRISES THE TOTAL 1975 STAFFING AND WORKLOAD. MAINTAINS PBX EQUIPMENT, CALL DIRECTOR, KEYSET AND INSTRUMENT EQUIPMENT 2 SHIFTS. INSTALLS, MOVES, REMOVES KEYSETS AND INSTRUMENTS 2 SHIFTS.

ALTERNATIVE WAYS OF PERFORMING WORK OR PROGRAM AND COSTS

BECAUSE SUPERVISION AND PBX MAINTENANCE CAPABILITY ARE COMBINED, NO LOWER COST ALTERNATIVE IS DISCERNABLE. HOWEVER, DELETING SWING SHIFT MAINTENANCE AND INSTALLATION WOULD REQUIRE ONE LESS PERSON FOR THIS PACKAGE AT A SAVING OF $15,000 AND INCREASE AVERAGE RESPONSE TIME FOR WORKING INSTRUMENT AND KEY EQUIPMENT ORDERS FROM 2 TO 16 DAYS.

ADVANTAGES OF RETAINING ACTIVITY

PERMITS MAINTENANCE OF PBX EQUIPMENT TO HOLD AVERAGE DIAL TONE DELAY TO 5 SECONDS OR LESS, MINIMIZING CALLER INCONVENIENCE, AND PERMITS MOST INSTRUMENT AND KEY EQUIPMENT INSTALL, MOVE OR REMOVE ORDERS TO BE WORKED DURING SWING-SHIFT HOURS WITH MINIMUM INCONVENIENCE TO OFFICE AND PROFESSIONAL EMPLOYEES.

CONSEQUENCES IF ACTIVITY IS ELIMINATED

TOTAL ELIMINATION OF THIS ACTIVITY WOULD RESULT IN REDUCED MAINTENANCE LEADING TO AVERAGE DIAL TONE DELAYS OF 30 SECONDS OR MORE WITHIN 6 MONTHS AND INCREASED RESPONSE TIME FOR KEY EQUIPMENT AND INSTRUMENT ORDERS FROM 2 TO 20 WORKING DAYS. ORDERS COULD BE WORKED ONLY DURING DAY SHIFT.

4. The listing illustrated below represents a priority ranking of decision packages at a divisional level.

PRIORITY RANKING   Date __AUGUST 15, 1975__

DEPARTMENT	DIVISION		PREPARED RALPH SCHWARTZ	PAGE 1
COMMUNICATIONS	CENTRAL		APPROVED B. MILLER	OF 1

	ACTIVITY				CURRENT YEAR (75)		BUDGET YEAR (76)		
RANK	NAME AND DESCRIPTION	LEVEL NO.	OF NO.	ORG. OBJ. NO.	PERSONNEL	$ (000)	PERSONNEL	$ (000)	CUMULATIVE $ (000)
1	PBX MAINTENANCE AND SUBSET INSTALLATIONS	1	3		4	60	4	63	63
2	TRUNKING MAINTENANCE	1	2		2	30	2	32	95
3	PBX OPERATIONS	1	2		6	72	6	77	172
4	DIRECTORY AND PAGING SERVICES	1	2		1	12	1	13	185
5	PBX MAINTENANCE AND SUBSET INSTALLATIONS	2	3		2	30	2	32	217
6	TRUNKING MAINTENANCE	2	2		1	15	1	16	233
7	PBX OPERATIONS	2	2		3	36	3	39	272
8	EQUIPMENT ENGINEERING	1	2		2	40	2	44	316
9	PBX MAINTENANCE AND SUBSET INSTALLATIONS	3	3		0	0	2	16	332
10	EQUIPMENT ENGINEERING	2	2		1	20	1	22	354
11	DIRECTORY AND PAGING SERVICES	2	2		1	12	1	13	367
	TOTALS				23	327	25	367	

5. The priority ranking continues with each higher level manager or officer merging and reranking lower priority packages for all organizations reporting to him.

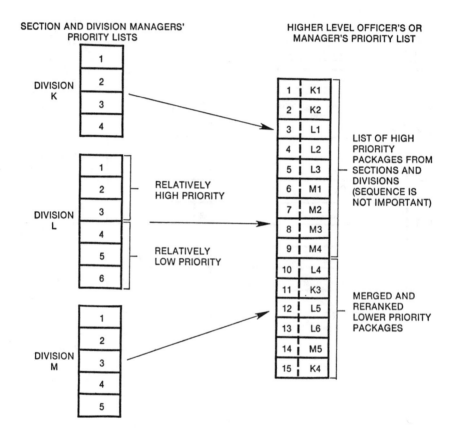

6. The objective is one companywide list of prioritized decision packages as illustrated in the chart below. Thus the chief administrative officer or a management committee reviews the rankings of senior officers and managers in terms of corporate needs and establishes individual department and total company budget levels.

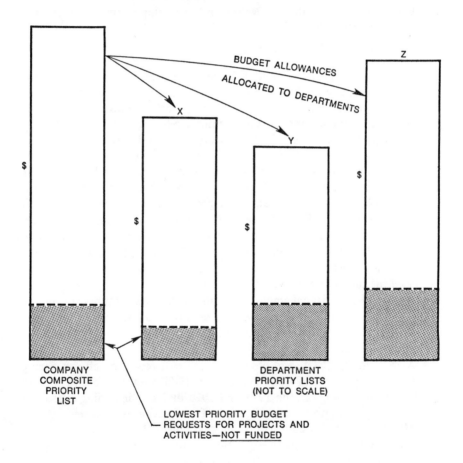

BUDGET ALLOWANCES ALLOCATED TO DEPARTMENTS

COMPANY COMPOSITE PRIORITY LIST

DEPARTMENT PRIORITY LISTS (NOT TO SCALE)

LOWEST PRIORITY BUDGET REQUESTS FOR PROJECTS AND ACTIVITIES—NOT FUNDED

An All-Out Test

The 1974 experience with ZBOP demonstrated that only a full-scale implementation of ZBOP would highlight nonessential and discretionary crabgrass activities sufficiently to permit selective cultivation of the entire operations and maintenance budget. Accordingly, the ZBOP process was extended throughout the entire company during 1975, and managers used it with varying degrees of success. At least one more annual cycle will be required to achieve a uniform level of understanding of its usefulness and to attain a corresponding high level of achievement. We can point, however, to some examples of significant progress:

- In preparing their 1975 and 1976 programs, each manager reporting to an officer analyzed all of his proposed activities in terms of continued need, relative contributions to the corporation, consequences if not funded, personnel and dollars required, and priority. These decision packages were then prioritized and summarized on ranking forms.
- Each officer reviewed the packages and ranks of each of his managers and assured himself that they were reasonable. As a final step, he merged and reranked the lowest priority activities of all his managers and forwarded his documentation through the corporate budget staff (for screening and summarization) to the Management Committee. During a two-day working session last December, the Management Committee met with each officer and department head to review the zero-base documentation and set an authorized personnel and funding level for each in 1976.
- Although the Management Committee scanned summaries of all activities, discussion centered on the details of lowest priority programs since these were the most likely candidates for deletion, postponement, or de-emphasis during budget year 1976.
- As a result of ZBOP and other on-going cost-reduction efforts during the latter part of 1974 and throughout 1975, we were able to achieve significant savings in the 1975 and 1976 budgets, including personnel reductions of approximately 9 percent from previously budgeted figures. Many of these reductions provided permanent dollar savings that will continue into future years—but only if the deleted crabgrass activities are not permitted to reseed and grow back in some other form.
- While many managers have come to appreciate the usefulness of ZBOP in planning and budgeting their own areas of responsibility, it appears the most significant utility of the process is at the middle and lower ranks of management. This is because the operating detail

produced during the development of the zero-base data is a useful working guide during the budget year itself.

* Because they knew ZBOP documentation gives senior management an opportunity to scrutinize operations in more depth than ever before, a number of managers deleted or scaled down certain activities in their proposed budget requests before submitting them to the Management Committee.

On the other hand, requiring managers to evaluate cost-effective alternatives has encouraged some to propose an increased level of spending for the budget year because they could demonstrate a compelling cost benefit or operational benefit in the near- or long-term. After candid discussion of the proposed increases, most were approved by the committee. In the absence of zero-base documentation, such proposed increases would have rarely survived senior management review in a period of fiscal restraint.

Future Expectations

Southern California Edison's use of the ZBOP process thus far has concentrated on identifying potential areas for budget reductions because of the need for general fiscal holddowns. But this represents only a partial use of the power of the process; equally as valuable is the use of ZBOP as a flexible planning-budgeting tool that permits managers to respond quickly and effectively to improvements in the business climate.

Having pre-planned, costed, and prioritized activities at hand, a. manager is equipped to proceed with additional cost-effective activities in support of company objectives should additional funds become available. We expect this aspect of the process to become increasingly useful as the company experiences an upturn in business activity.

Guidelines for Getting Started in ZBOP

For ZBOP to work, managers must be convinced there is something in it for them. After all, they will be asked to devote time to learning the concept—plus much additional time and effort in doing what is required to come up with an acceptable operating plan and budget. If they can't see some worthwhile benefits downstream, don't expect them to grasp ZBOP to their bosoms even if it does seem compellingly logical and appropriate to its advocates.

Long-range or strategic planning should precede the zero-base budgeting cycle. ZBOP concentrates on development of the operating budget, while long-range planning focuses on the general direction and development of the organization. Long-range planning should provide the goals, policy guidance, and assumptions for the zero-base process; zero-base should provide the first year's operating budget within the planning framework and should identify any conflicts between long-range goals and short-range growth and cost-reduction opportunities.

Most operating managers support a zero-base approach, especially during periods of severe budget reductions because ZBOP avoids a flat percentage reduction. But it also should be recognized that some managers will oppose any process that forces them to display their effectiveness and justify what they are doing. To overcome this problem, management support is needed.

It should be emphasized that ZBOP cannot be applied to an entire budget; it can be used for operations and programs over which management has some descretion. In the utility industry, for example, the zero-base approach can be used to develop budgets for administrative and general support, marketing, research, engineering, maintenance, construction and fabrication support, and some plant additions. It cannot be used for direct labor, direct material, and some direct overhead typically budgeted through "standard costing" procedures.

Tailoring Procedures to "Management Style"

The zero-base process encourages—indeed, it requires—a grassroots, bottoms-up approach to operations planning that necessitates the involvement of managers at all levels of the organization. If the process is followed faithfully and repeated each year, the positive benefits in terms of managerial effectiveness and organizational performance are impressive. The key to developing a tough-minded, professional spirit among managers lies in the simple fact that the zero-base process requires them to critically analyze, plan, adjust, and control their organizations in a way that brings their authority and responsibility into clear focus.

The process also requires an adjustment of the attitudes and perhaps even the managerial style of managers and their bosses. These adjustments are sometimes painful; not everyone can make the necessary transition successfully. But if the continued viability of a company is at stake, senior management is generally eager to make certain adjustments and sacrifices for themselves, to require the same of their subordinate managers, and through active, visible leadership bring about the required shift in managerial thrust.

No Panacea, But Worth a Trial Run

ZBOP is not an optimal answer to every manager's prayer for a simple effective operational planning and budgeting system, but it comes about as close as any. It is not for every organization or every manager in an organization, but it can produce cost-effective results in most segments of most organizations. An added advantage is that the zero-base approach sometimes can highlight deeply rooted management problems not related to zero-base itself.

The SCE experience indicates it is best to make a trial run in a small, representative organization for one full budget cycle. You assess these results, then either drop the idea completely or make necessary fine-tuning adjustments and implement it throughout the remainder of the organization where, from the perspective of senior management, it has a high probability of success.

Key to Success: Tough-Minded Managers

The ZBOP process can be adopted by virtually any organization willing to aggressively eliminate its budgetary crabgrass, but only tough-minded managers intimately acquainted with the organization culture can make it work effectively. Although the process is ideally suited for cost-effective planned growth, most managers probably will be initially interested in its enduring cost-reduction aspects and the capability it provides for responding flexibly to sudden shifts in an operating environment.

The final test of the net value of ZBOP is the way it is viewed by senior management. If, in spite of the time, cost, and anguish expressed by some managers, senior managers believe that on balance a lasting, significant benefit has been achieved, what more can be desired?

ZERO-BASE BUDGETING: A COMPARISON WITH TRADITIONAL BUDGETING*

Introduction

Zero-base Budgeting (ZBB) is an important budgetary process that is attracting interest in both the public and private sectors. It zoomed into prominence with the election of President Jimmy Carter and, at the present time, a number of corporations and governments are either using it or considering its introduction.

The traditional operating budgeting process may vary from being a totally dictated budget from top management downward to lower management with virtually no participation to a totally participative budget by lower management—a bottom-to-top approach. ZBB requires tremendous time and effort from lower and middle management and is extremely participative in nature. The purpose of this article is to compare the mechanical and behavioral aspects of the traditional operational budgeting process which uses a participative approach with ZBB. Since ZBB is used primarily for expenditures in the service and support areas, our discussion will be restricted to these areas. At this time it is not clear to what extent ZBB can be applied to factory overhead.

Traditional Participative Approach

The mechanical approach to both methods is somewhat similar. The manager who is responsible for implementing a budget is primarily responsible for preparing the budget. The format, detail, and emphasis of preparing the budget are different for ZBB and the traditional approach and, as a result, the method used to decide on the budget level of expenditures also varies.

Guidelines, which may be used by a manager responsible for preparing a budget, are usually established and passed down from a budget committee. The guidelines present current thinking about conditions which could affect a budget. They may include expected general economic trends, anticipated sales and production levels, format changes, anticipated supply availability, and any information considered relevant for a given area of responsibility.

---

*Reprinted from *Cost and Management* by Harper A. Roehm and Joseph F. Castellano by permission of Society of Industrial Accountants of Canada, Hamilton, Ontario, Canada, © November-December 1976.

Using guidelines provided by the budget committee, a manager prepares his budget for the coming fiscal period. A budget usually represents his intended expenditure level from which his performance will be evaluated. The budget should incorporate also his goals and objectives.

Since a manager often is competing for limited funds, he frequently builds "slack" into his budget. Slack may serve several needs. A manager may use it in negotiating his funding level during the budget approval process or he may use it to forfeit requested funds without sacrificing primary goals. If funds later become restricted, a manager may use his built-in-slack to cut funds from operations without really disturbing his overall operations. Finally, if budget cuts are not later required, he may use his slack to reduce actual cost and manipulate his actual cost to compare favorably to budget costs and, as a result, obtain a favorable performance report.

Typically, a manager's budget will begin with the current level of operations and will be adjusted upwards because of an anticipated higher operation level or because of additional goals and objectives. Following the initial budget preparation by each department, the budget director coordinates all budgets for the budget committee. Depending on the extent to which budget requests exceed anticipated funding levels, negotiations are conducted until a final budget is established.

The negotiation process may involve issues which could include budget slack, the goals and objectives, interpretations of how the budget committee's guidelines impact on a specific budget, the general efficiency of the department, and implementation of goals and objectives. Typically, there is not a prescribed negotiation procedure nor is there any structure to the process.

Zero-Base Budgeting Approach

The ZBB process also requires that a budget committee provide guidelines and coordinate overall efforts. There are two primary steps to ZBB. First "decision packages" must be formulated and second all of the decision packages must be ranked.

In formulating decision packages, each manager must identify within his area of responsibility specific activities which have identifiable costs. The sum total of the activities would represent a manager's total responsibility and total costs. Each activity should be associated with particular goals or objectives which would enable a manager to compare the activity's cost with its benefit and allow him to evaluate the activity's contribution—a cost/benefit analysis. For example, a manager of a cost department may perform the following functions:

1. Develop standard costs for inventory.
2. Maintain inventory records.
3. Compute and analyze inventory variances.
4. Prepare cost estimates for bids.
5. Perform various cost analyses associated with inventory.

Once a manager has spelled out these activities, he should identify the specific objectives and current cost associated with each.

In setting costs, a manager must determine for each decision package (i.e., standard cost for inventory, maintain inventory records, etc.) the minimum level of operations for that activity which is always assumed to be at a level lower than current expenditures. For example, in the function "maintenance of inventory records," a cost department may currently maintain most of the inventory on a perpetual system. The manager of a cost department may decide that the minimum level of operations and expenditures for this function would require that some inventory items currently on a perpetual basis should be maintained on a periodic inventory method.

After defining a minimum level of effort for a given function, a manager should develop alternative levels of performance and the costs associated with these additional levels. Continuing with the inventory example, the manager may have in addition to the minimum level any number of additional levels. Let us assume three more levels. The first level would put the firm back to current operations and the second and third would require all inventory to be maintained on a perpetual basis. The manager must identify the costs associated with each level of activity. Each additional effort represents a separate and distinct decision package. After a manager has determined minimum levels of effort for each activity and the additional effort levels, he ranks all his decision packages in order of decreasing importance. The manager must base his ranking on the guideline provided to him by the budget committee, top management, and his perception of the general function and importance of the department within the company as a whole.

Depending upon his instructions and guidelines provided to him, he may recommend that certain activities (decision packages) be eliminated or added. His charge may be to reduce costs by a certain percentage. He may be told to reduce operations to the minimum level with little guidance or he may be advised to prepare decision packages with no specific costs recommended.

The initial manager's rankings are then passed forward to his immediate supervisor who combines the decision packages of all those managers responsible to him into one ranking. The process continues until the final product is one ranking for the entire company. If budget cuts are necessary, those decision packages with the lowest priorities for the company as a whole are eliminated. As noted earlier in the perpetual inventory example, each manager also prepares packages beyond his current level of operations so that if additional funds are available, these funds will be used on those packages with the highest priority.

One final comment should be made about the mechanical aspects of ZBB. As the packages are ranked at each level and passed upwards through the organization's structure, different levels of participation may be allowed in the ranking process. A supervising manager may allow his subordinate manager to vote on the overall ranking or he may decide on the other extreme and perform the ranking entirely on his own without any participation. A supervising manager may first rank all decision packages and then allow some negotiation with his subordinates. There are many alternatives available. Top management should provide a ranking policy before initiating ZBB.

Comparison of Mechanical Aspects

Both budget procedures require guidelines from higher levels of management; both require extensive participation by lower level management; both allow for negotiations; however, there are significant differences. Essentially ZBB requires a manager to define more clearly his tasks and the associated costs.

The advocates of ZBB stress the importance of clear and precise budgetary guidelines from top management as a prerequisite. While this requirement is no less important under a traditional budgetary process, the implications of not providing these assumptions are more striking because of the emphasis placed upon: (1) the preparation of decision packages at various levels of effort and, (2) the necessity of ranking decision packages. For example, perpetual inventory systems often permit companies to provide better customer service and to reduce their investment in inventory. In order for an inventory manager to recommend converting some inventory records previously maintained on a perpetual basis to a periodic method, he must have a very clear understanding of top management's priorities in regard to products, markets, and customers. In addition, the ranking process will require a set of criteria which would not be absolutely essential under the traditional budgeting approach.

Finally, the initial preparation of ZBB requires more time, involvement, and effort. As indicated earlier, lower level managers must identify decision packages, minimum levels of effort and additional levels of effort, recommend cost reductions, and rank packages. A traditional approach to budgeting usually requires a manager to recommend a budget with justification for only additional (incremental) expenditures. The budget is usually not prepared in a decision package format and does not involve as much structure and detail as that required in ZBB. The conversion to a ZBB process usually is more time consuming in the first year than a traditional budget process but typically involves far less time in the second and succeeding years.

Behavioral Aspects of Participative Budgeting

Much has been written about the behavioral aspects of the participative approach to budgeting and only a brief review will be presented here. The participative approach to budgeting encourages managers to plan, improve coordination and communication, provides a bench mark which may be used to evaluate performance and facilitates decentralized performance measurement.

Decentralization is a popular management style where decisions are to be made at the level of management where they are to be implemented. As a result the decision-making process is enhanced. Participative budgeting allows lower level managers to be involved in establishing their own goals and is considered an integral part of a decentralized management. This is an important part of the process for when a manager participates in setting his department's objectives, he is more apt to "internalize" these objectives as his own. Department goals become personal goals and, as a result, this goal congruence is likely to lead to an increase in motivation.

The Behavioral Aspects of ZBB

ZBB is more participative than traditional participative budgeting. The question is: Does ZBB's greater involvement by managers change any of the behavioral aspects of participative budgeting? Are there improvements? Since ZBB is a relatively new phenomenon, researchers have not yet answered these questions; however, ZBB proponents and observers believe that it has behavioral advantages over a traditional participative budgeting process. Four observations will be made.

First, because ZBB requires more involvement, requires functions and associated costs to be more clearly identified, criteria more precisely spelled out, and all functions ranked, the chances are greater that ZBB will achieve the behavioral objectives of participative budgeting. These objectives are better planning, coordination and communication, better performance evaluation, a more effective decision making process, and greater goal congruency.

Second, although a required objective of ZBB is not necessarily cost reduction, ZBB appears to be more oriented toward cost reduction than the traditional approach to participative management. A manager is measured in part on how effectively he can identify a minimum level for each activity. The ranking of packages implies that, if necessary, some functions must be eliminated. ZBB proponents feel that, as a result of this atmosphere, ZBB tends to reduce the amount of slack built into budgets. This has not been proven or tested.

Third, ZBB provides more intrinsic rewards and motivation. It is generally believed that intrinsic rewards cannot be mandated by an organization but must originate and be felt within a person. They are controlled and perceived by the individual and can be a powerful form of motivation. Usually corporations can affect intrinsic motivation by how they structure the work environment.

Generally behavioralists believe that when a job enables a participant to feel personally responsible for a meaningful portion of the task more intrinsic motivation results. A manager must believe that whatever successes or failures occur are a result of his efforts. Certainly ZBB is more individually task-oriented and has the characteristics to enable a manager to feel more personally responsible for his performance.

Finally, ZBB provides a more rational approach for adding new projects or eliminating functions when cost reductions are required. Managers should feel better about the selection of new projects since the ranking process should instill the perception of a "fair game." In fact, a controller of a large Fortune 500 corporation which recently implemented ZBB told of a manager volunteering to resign after seeing where his areas of responsibility ranked. The controller felt that if any other process had been used, ill will between the manager and the company may have resulted.

Summary

ZBB is an alternative to the traditional participative approach to budgeting. If a firm wants the advantages of ZBB, it must have some degree of participative budgeting and decentralization. Even within this framework there are degrees of participation especially during the ranking process.

Generally ZBB may be characterized as a method requiring more of everything: more work, more involvement, more participation. Hopefully, this additional commitment will result in better planning, communication, performance measurement and decision making. In addition, ZBB should reduce the element of slack in budgets and provide a more rational approach to cost reduction and new project selection.

Chapter 3

The Design and Development of Decision Packages

The first step the chief fiscal officer (CFO) must take when implementing a zero-base budgeting system is to identify the units of the facility that will be responsible for preparing the decision packages. This step is important because, among other considerations, if the CFO picks a management level too low in the organization, the number of decision packages will be far too voluminous. On the other hand, if the management level is too high, valuable detail will be lost in the aggregation. Once the management levels have been established, the CFO must design the forms and develop procedures the preparers can follow. Poor form design and procedures may result in inadequate information or decision packages that cannot be compared, which will make the ranking process ineffectual or impossible. CFOs must make these decisions in the contexts of their health care facilities. This chapter investigates two areas that may assist the CFOs' decisions. The first section focuses on selecting the proper level in the organization for preparation of decision packages. The second section covers the form design and procedures for developing a decision package.

CHOOSING THE ORGANIZATIONAL LEVEL

A general rule is to choose the management level to prepare decision packages that will give the administration the best information for resource allocation and control without its being overwhelmed with detail. A health care facility's administration could request all persons below the level of a department head who are responsible for projects or programs to submit decision packages for their areas. The results may be positive, or the packages may justify partial employees (1/8 FTE) or small dollar expenditures. However, the number of packages may be too large to evaluate since they may increase geometrically. If a department head, for example, were to submit four packages, the four subunit supervisors might submit three packages each, or 12 in all. Decision packages covering small areas of responsibility tend to be too numerous to evaluate subjectively.

On the other hand, an administrator may have three assistant administrators who are responsible for functional areas of the hospital. Requiring the three administrators to prepare decision packages for their areas would result in a loss of valuable information that would be generated farther down the organizational hierarchy. Fewer decision packages would result, but information for resource allocation would be limited severely. The management level established in the health care institution responsible for package preparation should be flexible to gain maximum benefits. Several considerations should be observed before delegating the preparation duties to specific management levels in the health care institution:

- the level of management where meaningful decisions can be made
- the size of the institution
- the time available for package preparation and ranking
- the alternatives available

Level of Management

The hospital's organizational chart may be the best place to begin isolating decision package preparers. Cost centers should be identified on the chart, since they were established to control basic activities. The cost centers would include housekeeping, maintenance, nursing, and administration, among others. The manager of each cost center may desire to develop packages for that level or break out functional elements within the center. The maintenance department, for example, may have automotive, grounds, external maintenance, and internal maintenance as functional subunits. Each subunit could be required to prepare packages. Another alternative is to consolidate two or more cost centers and prepare packages for the combination. Several nursing units may be combined, rather than preparing packages for each one.

Size of the Institution

The size of the hospital or institution will influence the development of decision packages. A dietary department may have the functions of food preparation, patient rounds, diet preparation, and consulting patients. These functions are common in many hospitals, regardless of their size. However, the hospital's size does affect the number of staff persons necessary to carry out these functions. One hospital may have one registered dietitian responsible for all functions and a staff of five. Another may have a staff of 20 food preparers and several registered dietitians, each responsible for a functional area, with a chief coordinating the department. In the smaller hospital, the department with one dietitian would have no alternative but to prepare decision packages excluding professional staff.

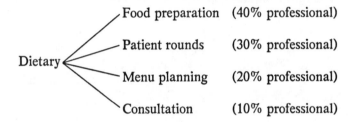

Dietary

Food preparation   (40% professional)

Patient rounds   (30% professional)

Menu planning   (20% professional)

Consultation   (10% professional)

Decision packages prepared for patient rounds, menu planning, and consultation would be of no value since all functions are assumed necessary and only one professional is available. Elimination of a percentage of time results in no reduction of staff or dollar savings. Food preparation, on the other hand, may be broken into packages for analysis of the food preparation staff. A minimum package always would include one professional staff member.

For the larger hospital, the professional staff might be assigned this way:

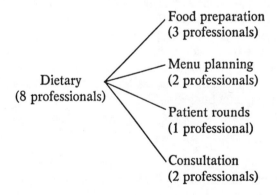

Dietary
(8 professionals)

Food preparation
(3 professionals)

Menu planning
(2 professionals)

Patient rounds
(1 professional)

Consultation
(2 professionals)

The larger staff of professionals allows packages to be developed that can show the effects of whole-person staff reduction. A minimum package might show the following:

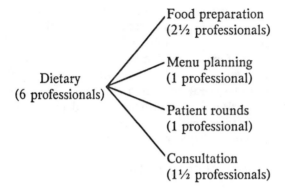

Even with the same identifiable functional areas, the two hospitals would prepare packages differently because of professional staff size. The larger the institution, the more divisible the activities will be if packages are to be developed around people costs.

Time Available

Any budgeting system will take staff time for preparation. The time available for assembling decision packages in a ZBB system will influence the selection of areas in the organization for preparation. More time is necessary for preparing packages for functional areas within cost centers than for the cost centers as a whole. Furthermore, it will take more time to prepare under the ZBB process in the first year than in subsequent years. One company reported that the time required in the second year for ZBB was about half that of the first year, and slightly less in the third year.

For health care institutions with unclear lines of authority and responsibility because of deficient organizational planning and policies, the time required may be substantial. In addition, an institution that has been using an authoritarian or "top-down" budget may require considerable time and effort from department managers because they have not developed and exercised planning and budgeting skills.

Alternatives Available

Another consideration when assigning the development of decision packages is the availability of alternative solutions to the problem. For some cost centers in an institution there may be no available alternatives because of union contracts, lease agreements, regulatory requirements, or legal implications. If the hospital is under a long-term contract with a laundry firm, the terms may include a substantial penalty for cancellation.

The administration may have no alternative such as installing in-house laundry facilities until the contract expires. A nursing home operator may have no option for reducing the cost of a registered dietitian or medical librarian because Medicare regulations require that each home have the services of these professionals before it can qualify for Medicare reimbursements. Identification of these nonalternative areas is important because the passage of time may change the situations so that alternatives become available. Identification will enable management to react quickly and take advantage of changes.

FOCUS OF DECISION PACKAGES

Once the decision package preparers have been identified, the administration must clarify the meaning of a discrete activity for the focus of the package. Preparers will want to know how to segment their areas of responsibility so they can develop meaningful packages covering these segments. A decision unit generally is thought of as a basic activity or group of activities that the administration considers for planning, analysis, and review. The decision unit can be a cost center, a program, or a capital expenditure, among others. In most health care institutions, the following may be subjects of decision packages:

- people
- cost or revenue centers
- programs and projects
- accounting line items
- capital expenditures

Two items for the preparers to consider: (1) the decision packages may include more than one of the above subjects, (i.e., a capital expenditure that requires additional personnel) but only one of the two or more subjects will be the center of attention; and (2) the subject of the packages is not as important as the benefits expected from the additional resources spent. The preparers must apply careful thought when analyzing decision units. Each decision package subject listed above will be discussed briefly.

People

In many health care institutions, people will be the subjects of some decision packages. This is because (1) health care is labor intensive, (2) most operating costs are people related, (3) some people can be identified with specific tasks, and (4) some people can perform several tasks, which allows for consolidating activities and eliminating unneeded personnel. An example of people-related decision packages might be those submitted by the manager of patient accounts (Exhibit 2-1 in Chapter 2).

Cost Centers

Cost centers probably are the decision units used most by industry and government because they can be identified easily through the organization chart. For many health care facilities, cost centers may be the first choice because of convenience, since they may have been used as focal points in more traditional budgeting systems. Cost centers may be broken down by functional area by the department head, as discussed earlier in this chapter.

Programs and Projects

Programs and projects are identified readily as decision units and often are the subjects of decision packages. Since alternatives generally are available, packages can be developed for several levels of activity or for different ways of accomplishing the project's objectives.

A hospital may wish, for example, to install a home health care unit as a part of its organization. The alternatives available may be to contract a local home health agency, to establish a freestanding unit under the hospital's administration, or to abandon the idea. The hospital also must consider levels of funding and staffing if an in-house unit is selected. Partial personnel (fractions of staff-months or staff-years) may be included in the decision packages if personnel can be shared with other programs. However, if a program needs a fractional person at a minimum decision level, for example 1 ¾ staff-years of time, and that fractional person is not approved, the program could be scrapped and other programs that were allocated the remaining time could be affected. Under a project orientation approach, the packages would have characteristics similar to those oriented toward cost centers in that each package should identify funding necessary for personnel costs, medical supplies, administrative supplies, equipment, travel, and other line item costs.

Accounting Line Items

Some decision packages will involve expenditures by objective or by accounting line items that often are under administrative control. These could include legal costs, certain leasing arrangements, and contributions.

Most accounting line items can be identified with a cost center or allocated among several centers and should be projected by the lower level of management.

Capital Expenditures

Major capital expenditures can be made the subjects of decision packages, just as programs and projects are. Minor capital expenditures should be included in the packages of other subjects. Capital expenditure packages are advantageous because management can evaluate and rank them along with packages covering people, projects, or other subjects. Management can analyze the potential effects on cash flow for current and future periods and the capital item's effectiveness if partial funding is allowed or additional funding is made available. Decision packages on capital expenditures provide an excellent vehicle for post-completion audits, especially if the expenditure is made to provide benefits not measurable in terms of cash flow.

A major capital expenditure decision package for a new wing for a nursing home facility might include:

Exhibit 3-1   Sample Decision Package for Hospital Expansion

Decision Package—South Wing Expansion
Capital outlay (millions)

	Current Year	Second Year	Third Year
• Capital expenditure costs	$1.8	$.60	$.200
• Depreciation		.09	.093

Benefits: Expansion from 40 beds to 70 beds; provide additional common area space; provide 10 more private rooms for residents and 20 rooms for double occupancy. Expansion designed to meet increased applications for occupancy and anticipated elderly population growth of locale.

Alternatives:
- Add fewer than 30 beds.
- Postpone addition until population growth patterns and age compositions are known better.
- Change room accommodations to fewer private rooms and more double occupancy.

- Limit the common area.
- Postpone addition until later in current year to shift cash outflow to subsequent years.

Decision packages for this example would show the funding necessary and expected consequences for each alternative listed. Furthermore, management has greater adaptability when alternatives are presented in the form of decision packages. The effects of postponements can be anticipated if, for example, bond issues are slow to sell or other financial problems arise.

FORMULATING DECISION PACKAGES

Two alternatives are available for developing decision packages that should be understood by the budget supervisor and communicated to the preparers:

1. Different methods of performing the same function (mutually exclusive packages): Mutually exclusive packages identify alternatives for performing the same function. The best method is chosen, but the alternative methods should be identified in the decision package along with a brief explanation of why they were not chosen. If an alternative to the present method of performing the function is selected, the present method should be shown as an alternative.
2. Different levels of effort in performing the function (incremental packages): Incremental packages identify alternatives for different levels of effort to perform a specific function. A minimum level of effort is established, but additional levels of effort are identified as separate decision packages. This minimum level of effort may not completely achieve the purpose of the function but should identify and attack the most important elements. In most cases, the minimum level of effort will be below the current level of expenditures. The minimum level package should be ranked higher than the additional packages to assure approval.*

Information Contained in Format

The ZBB process will require an information/time trade-off. The more information required of the decision package preparer, the more time will

---

*Reprinted from "An Evaluation of the Zero-Base Budgeting System in Governmental Institutions" by George S. Minmier by permission of Georgia State University, © 1975.

be needed to obtain it. There may be an exponential relationship between additional information and additional time; for example, 10 percent more information may require 30 percent more time to obtain it. Several questions should be asked to establish the quantity of information to be included in packages:

- How much time can be allocated to information gathering?
- What is the minimum amount of information necessary for proper evaluation and ranking?
- How meaningful will incremental information be to the evaluation and ranking process?

The information requirements for each package should be flexible to allow department heads to modify their inputs to meet their needs. Some consistency in the information is necessary for comparison purposes. The administration of each health care facility must design the format and information requirements to meet its needs. Information in each package may range from broad categories to more detailed items. Figure 3-1 illustrates this degree of detail. Even though the information on package forms may vary somewhat in amounts of detail, the following categories are found in most packages:

- general information
- description of purpose and program
- benefits
- alternatives
- costs

Each one of these categories is described below.

General Information

The general information should allow the reader to identify the package easily. The information should include, among other data, the package name or title, its rank, date of preparation, and organizational identification. The package name should refer to the kind of project or program involved and the level of effort the package covers (minimum, current, additional levels). Other information could include the name of the department manager or the preparer, the name of the immediate superior, the telephone extension, and the work shift.

The form may contain space for the rank number. This number identifies the rank of the decision package compared to all other packages being

Figure 3-1 Information That May Be in Decision Packages

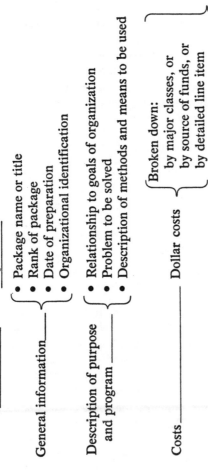

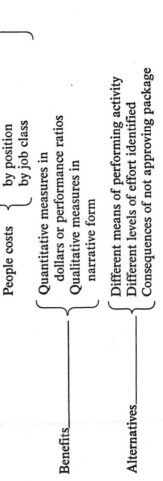

Broad Areas — Specifics

General information
• Package name or title
• Rank of package
• Date of preparation
• Organizational identification

Description of purpose and program
• Relationship to goals of organization
• Problem to be solved
• Description of methods and means to be used

Costs — Dollar costs
Broken down:
by major classes, or
by source of funds, or
by detailed line item

People costs
Broken down:
by position
by job class

Time of expenditure:
Past year(s)
Current year
Budget year(s)
Projections
Interim periods

Benefits
Quantitative measures in dollars or performance ratios
Qualitative measures in narrative form

Alternatives
Different means of performing activity
Different levels of effort identified
Consequences of not approving package

ranked at that organizational level. The ranking will change as the process moves toward the top administrative level and other packages are consolidated into the ratings.

The preparation date can assist the managers if the packages are revised. The date helps department heads and other management recognize the originals from subsequent packages. Exhibit 3-2 is an example of a package form that provides this general information.

Exhibit 3-2   Decision Package Form—Stage 1

Anytown Community Hospital

Decision package _3_ of _4_   Date prepared _3/14/79_

Decision Unit Name: Decision Unit Head
Medical Records   or Supervisor: *A. Rollins*
                                       Centrex Extension: _4210_

Department: *Patient Services*   This package is
                                           __ minimum level
Department Head: *S. Compton*   __ normal level
                                           ✓ additional level
Centrex Extension: _____   __ other (explain)

Purpose or activity description:

Benefits:

Alternatives:

Costs (detail may be attached on separate sheet):

Consequences of not funding:

Description of Purpose and Program

This section of the decision package will answer such questions as:

- How does this activity relate to the objectives of the whole organization?
- From the description of the purpose and program, will the administration clearly understand the package and identify its contributions with the total organization?
- Will the purpose and program as described conform with the policies of the administration?

The section on purpose and program may be expanded or contracted, depending on how well department heads understand their goals and objectives vis-a-vis the organization's. The extent of this section's development depends on the department heads' understanding of their function's role and its interaction with other elements of the organization. The less department managers understand or are aware of these interrelationships, the more time and form space management should devote to their explanation. One of the values of ZBB is to give lower level managers an appreciation of the teamwork necessary to accomplish the facility's objectives. All too often department heads' concerns and interests rest solely with their own unit and its intraworkings. Little or no concern is given to other departments unless there are complaints to be heard. For some health care facilities, separate sections for Description of Purpose and Description of Activities would be advisable. Other facilities may find Description of Activity and Objectives of Activity to be appropriate separate sections. Still other facilities may wish to combine the two groupings into a single section. Exhibit 3-3 illustrates the first two sections completed.

Benefits

The cost/benefit relationships of decision packages are analyzed and decisions are made, often subjectively, as to which packages to fund and which not to fund. The keys to the decision are the cost/benefit justifications of each package. Benefits sometimes are much more difficult to assess than costs because (1) benefits are future values and costs often are present and (2) benefits may not be quantifiable in dollar terms to compare with costs.

The expected benefits of funding a package should be considered carefully as to whether they are realistic and what can be achieved. An overzealous department head may propose benefits that are unrealistic and cannot be delivered. During the evaluation process, rankings may be

Exhibit 3-3 Design Package Form—Stage 2

Anytown Community Hospital

Decision package _3_ of _4_   Date prepared _3/14/79_

Decision Unit Name:	Decision Unit Head
Medical Records	or Supervisor: _A. Rollins_
	Centrex Extension: _4210_
Department: _Patient Services_	This package is
	__ minimum level
Department Head: _S. Compton_	__ normal level
	_✓_ additional level
Centrex Extension: _____	__ other (explain)

Purpose or activity description:
Convert medical records kept prior to 7/1/76 to microfilm. Microfilming of medical records commenced 7/1/76.

Benefits:
Will release record space which under present conditions will require expansion of old space or the acquisition of presently unused hospital space. Released space will be adequate for 3 years.

Alternatives:
Unused hospital space for file storage is either non-existent or unsuitable due to lack of security. Expansion of existing space is described in package 4 of 4.

Costs (detail may be attached on separate sheet):
Decision Packages and Funding

Personnel	*$1,500*	*1 of 4*	*$26,840*
Supplies	*1,200*	*2 of 4*	*4,970*
Equipment (microfilm files)	*950*	*→3 of 4*	*3,650*
Total	*3,650*	*4 of 4*	*4,260*

Consequences of not funding:
Space must be found for medical records unit in present facility or expansion must be undertaken.

confused and funding may be provided to the package(s) with the unrealistic estimations. Unrealistic estimates can be prevented by holding the department head responsible for unmet claims. As mentioned in Chapter 1, the responsible manager should be given an opportunity to comment on or explain any differences between budgeted and actual inputs—or outputs. Events may have occurred that caused the difference to be beyond the manager's foresight and control.

Benefits should be quantified in terms suitable for performance measurement, even though they may not be quantified in dollars. Performance measurement is a useful tool for department heads to control their activities and ensure that resources are used efficiently and effectively. Generally, performance measures for health care institutions fall into two classes: productivity measurement and unit costs.

Productivity measurement measures the total output and compares this to the total resource input. Often this takes the form of a productivity index, which is a ratio of output divided by input. The output may be defined as the services performed for use outside by the organization or subunit. The productivity measure should be established so that comparisons can be drawn on a year-to-year basis. A home health care agency unit may have patients per day per nurse as a productivity index. A housekeeping department may establish a patient's room per day per staff as a productivity index.

Unit costs often are used as performance measurements. Costs per unit of output or service can be meaningful if inputs are quantifiable in terms of dollars. Food cost per patient meal is a performance measure subject to unit costing. Unit costs can be monitored as an objective measure of a unit's efficiency. A note of caution: unit costs can be misleading and can have significant negative impacts if used improperly. Some potential problems:

- Unit costs that contain both fixed and variable cost elements will vary because of changes in total costs *or* in volume of activity. In the example above, the food cost per patient meal is a variable cost. The varying of patient meals served will change the food cost, assuming waste is minimal. The unit cost should be stable over normal changes in volume of activity (See Figure 3-2). However, if the expenses of preparation and of food are desired as unit costs per meal served, a problem of interpretation arises. As more or fewer meals are served, the unit cost for preparation of each meal rises and falls as the fixed salary or wage costs are allocated (See Figure 3-3). An improper analysis of unit costs alone, as shown in Figure 3-3, may mislead the decision maker into believing costs are decreasing when in fact

Figure 3-2 Unit Food Costs Per Meal Served

	198^A	198^B
Food costs per year..................................	$ 57,745	$97,623
Meals served.......................................	102,750	150,190
Unit cost per meal..................................	.562	.65

Figure 3-3 Unit Food and Preparation Costs Per Meal Served

	198^A	198^B
Food costs per year..................................	$ 57,745	$ 97,623
Preparation costs...................................	56,000	58,000
Total costs..	$113,745	$155,623
Meals served.......................................	102,750	150,190
Unit cost per meal..................................	$ 1.107	$ 1.036

total expenses are increasing but being spread over a greater number of units.

- The use of unit costs may lead department heads to believe that in any trade-off between cost and quality of service, the quality of service would be the one to go. Department heads become concerned because they see the administration as very concerned about efficiency, but much less concerned about the effectiveness of their function.
- Similarly, department heads may view the unit cost as a highly inflexible measure that will not be altered as changes occur in their function or program.
- Finally, unit costs are only as good as the cost accumulation system. The cost accounting system must be able to generate meaningful unit expenses. The hospital's allocation of indirect costs to revenue producing departments must provide a fair and equitable distribution.

Regardless of the performance measurement method or the proved effectiveness of the department head, proposed accomplishments and benefits are difficult to define because they must be forecast. The benefits should relate as closely as possible to the package. This relationship often poses a problem in that the benefits are qualitative and would not accrue if that package were accepted without the approval of previous packages in the series.

Alternatives

This section of the package allows the preparer to consider, in written form, any alternate means of accomplishing the objective(s) of the decision package. The alternative section is very important in that the preparer is required to think of more than a single approach, and evaluate each, to arrive at the best method. Since preparers should be held responsible for areas of the proposal under their control, they will be careful not to take an alternative that is not the best just because they are biased in its favor.

This section also may contain summaries of the effects of different effort levels. If the package is numbered 3 of 4, a brief summary of the benefits and funding requirements may be presented for packages 1 of 4, 2 of 4, and 4 of 4. The administration will find this helpful when ranking projects since it probably is concerned about rating incremental levels above normal funding requirements. The summary is particularly helpful in large health care facilities when the administration has numerous packages to consider.

Finally, the alternative section may contain information on consequences of not funding the package. Again, the preparer must forecast some possible occurrences that should improve the planning process. The consequences may range from a reduction of service, to effects on other activities, to a violation of government regulation.

Costs

There is no question that costs should be included in the decision package since rankings will depend on cost/benefit relationships. The problem on cost information is how much or what degree of detail should be presented. Sufficient cost detail should be presented so the person or group evaluating the packages can make proper decisions. Certainly, a minimum of cost detail would include total additional expenses for the package to be funded and the accumulation of package costs if the package is part of a series. Other information considered valuable would include the number of people covered by the packages. After these two basic points, total money and number of people, additional information may be provided in various quantities. This information may be valuable to a point, but once that point is reached more information becomes meaningless or, worse, confusing. Detailed information has its advantages and disadvantages, such as:

1. Advantages of detail cost information on packages:
   a. Managers must do some detail estimating to obtain a good cost figure, so filling out the form may not take much additional effort.

    b. Top management can have greater confidence in a detailed cost estimate.

    c. Top management can modify the costs of each package more easily (such as changing travel, consulting fees, capital) while still approving the package.

    d. All required information can be obtained from one document.

2. Disadvantages of detail cost information on packages:

    a. Some packages will not be funded, so the extra effort on these packages will be wasted.

    b. Detailed information usually is required only at the cost center or budget unit level whose budget will be determined from several approved packages; therefore, the detail can be obtained for one unit rather than totaling the information from each decision package.

    c. Managers often want fine tuning and minor modifications after their funding levels are established, and they then would need to modify the detail costing obtained from the packages.

Some of the problems of detailed costing may be avoided by supplying basic expense information before funding and more detailed information can be added after a package is accepted. Some relevant information for the funding decision will be left out of the package, but the savings in time and effort of department heads and other preparers may be worth the reduction in detail.

Several considerations should be made during the deliberation of the proper cost information to include in decision packages:

- The cost information supplied and its adequacy for the health care facility should be appraised. Can it be utilized for decision package development?

- Since the primary decision is concerned with funding or not funding the package, adequate information for this decision is required. The amount may vary from facility to facility and within the facility from year to year.

- Additional data may be required after the funding decision so the administration and department heads can monitor the implementation, control, and follow-up phases.

- The cost information system should be evaluated according to its ability to meet the information needs. This process leads to consideration of modifying the present system and the benefits to be gained from that.

The decision package forms will dictate, to a large degree, the information to be generated by the preparer. The forms in the Appendix illustrate the variation in the amount of information that can be presented. In summary, the classification of expenses may be composed of one or more of the following:

- costs for the upcoming budget period only
- costs for the current year and/or past year and/or projections beyond the next budget year
- costs for interim periods, such as monthly or quarterly, of the upcoming budget period
- total dollars budgeted for the effort levels
- total dollars budgeted for the effort levels, differentiated by major expenditure classifications
- total dollars budgeted for the effort levels, differentiated by major and minor expenditure classifications
- total dollars budgeted for the effort levels, with internal costing mechanisms, including transfer changes or other allocations
- source of funds to cover the expenditures (grants, endowments, gifts)

CONTINUOUS PREPARATION OF DECISION PACKAGES

The preparation process should not end when the department managers complete their decision packages for the upcoming year's budget. Certainly the bulk of the package preparation has been completed, but new ideas, programs, and proposals continue to develop because the hospital and its environment are not static, independent entities. Even after the budget has reached its final form and is implemented as the institution's financial plan, managers should be alert for opportunities that can be converted to a decision package format and transmitted through the organizational hierarchy for review.

There are several reasons for continually developing and preparing decision packages. They are:

- Managers will have an outlet for innovative ideas which may otherwise be forgotten;
- It forces managers to "think through" the proposal and consider the potential benefits and costs (often the enthusiasm for an idea will wane when the expense of implementation is considered);
- Proposals that are submitted after the budget is completed will be

ranked along with other proposals, which were not funded initially, if additional resources become available;

- Decision packages prepared during budget periods will reduce the number of packages to be prepared immediately before the next budget.

Continuous decision package preparation is a concept that should be adopted by an institution using ZBB.

Chapter 4

The Ranking Process

The ranking process enables the administration to decide which decision packages should be funded and which should not. As the name implies, a listing of all packages is prepared, with priority units listed first and the others in order of descending priority. During this process, all those involved in the ranking process are considering the relative merits of the packages based on cost and benefit information supplied by the preparers. In most cases, not all packages will be funded because of capital limitations and because some will have cost/benefit relationships that make them unworthy of funding at this or any other time.

The health care facility's administration must consider two questions prior to the ranking process: (1) what funding will the institution be able to provide? and (2) corollary, will the institution generate sufficient revenue to cover the requests? Profit-oriented businesses generally answer the second question by forecasting sales or revenues first and then establishing expense estimates. The expense estimates form the basic budget requests. In contrast, many hospitals and other health facilities estimate costs and expenses first, then establish a revenue budget sufficient to cover estimated costs. This procedure is followed, in part, because Medicare requires reimbursement at cost or charge, whichever is lower. The hospital must take this and other legal requirements into consideration when establishing the revenue budget.

THE RANKING FORM FORMAT

The ranking form is designed to give management a convenient worksheet to ease the difficulties in ranking numerous packages. The form also provides the administration other benefits:

- a means of reviewing all packages quickly to see what types were considered most important in previous rankings

- an ability to observe quickly the funding requirements for this year's packages as compared to last year's budget. This advantage is useful especially when comparing funds required for the minimum effort in the coming year to those needed for normal operations last year. Dramatic increases in the minimum level of funding for certain packages in comparison to normal operations may cause the administration to subject those units to closer review to determine whether there are improper increases or reductions in the minimum levels of effort.
- added flexibility, in that different levels of funding may be applied to the rankings to determine which packages would be dropped or added if funds were expanded or contracted

The level of management using the ranking form should find it adaptable for the benefits above. Several formats may be used. One of these appears in Figure 2-2 and another in Figure 4-1. The form in Figure 2-2 requires that cumulative funding be shown, while the one in Figure 4-1 does not. The facility preparing to rank its packages should design the form in a manner that meets management's own purposes.

DEALING WITH THE VOLUME OF PACKAGES

Rankings begin at the lowest level of the management hierarchy. Subsequent ratings are conducted at higher levels until a single ranking is consolidated at the top management level. As the ranking progresses, management must sift through more and more packages. In a large hospital, for example, the chief radiologist may have six packages to rank for the radiology department but the administrator may have 200 to handle as the 40 departments and functions submit their evaluations. Figure 4-2 illustrates the problem of volume as the system progresses. Each department manager must rank packages initiated at that level. Further rankings take place as departments are grouped, by function or other criteria, and consolidated packages are listed according to priority. At the group level, the volume problem manifests itself. In Group IV, of which Radiology is part, there are 24 packages, which may seem numerous until compared to Group III, which has 76. Compared to the administrator who must evaluate 200 packages, the ranking problem at the group level seems almost insignificant.

There are two fundamental ways to cope with the volume of packages:

1. limit the number of levels of consolidation in the ranking process
2. establish a cutoff point above which packages will not be scrutinized as closely, allowing management to give more attention to marginal priority packages

Figure 4-1 Decision Package Ranking

Rank	Package name	Last year's budget			This year's budget			Cumulative level		
		Total funding	Hospital funding	FTE	Total funding	Hospital funding	FTE	Total funding	Hospital funding	Cum %
1	Dietary (1 of 4)	225	225	19	200	200	18	200	200	23
2	Radiology (1 of 2)	121	121	3	95	95	3	295	295	33
3	Nursing (1 of 2)	290	290	30	235	235	25	530	530	60
4	Physical Therapy (1 of 3)	131	131	11	109	109	10	639	639	73*
5	Pharmacy (1 of 3)	110	110	3	93	93	3	732	732	83
6	Physical Therapy (2 of 3)				14	14	1	746	746	85
7	Dietary (2 of 4)				16	16	1	762	762	87
8	Nursing (2 of 2)				50	45	5	812	807	92
9	Radiology (2 of 2)				20	20	0	832	827	94
10	Pharmacy (2 of 3)				16	16	1	848	843	96
11	Physical Therapy (3 of 3)				10	10	0	858	853	97
12	Dietary (3 of 4)				12	12	0	870	865	99
13	Dietary (4 of 4)				9	9	0	879	874	100
14	Pharmacy (3 of 3)				14	12	1	893	886	101

$$*\frac{\text{Cumulative hospital funding this year}}{\text{Total hospital funding last year}} = \frac{530}{877} = 73\%$$

Limiting the Number of Rankings

The process will continue until a single ranking is established for funding. Usually the institution can be broken down into convenient ranking levels by using the organization chart. Units, departments, cost centers, revenue centers, and divisions can be the levels. Each ranking and reranking takes significant time and effort. If rerankings can be limited to low management levels, time and cost savings will result. For example, rather than ranking and reranking at five levels of management, only two or three at low levels might suffice. A significant loss of management trade-off between packages will occur even though there may be a saving of time. The gaps between management levels doing the ranking will become great, with a corresponding loss of some intimate knowledge regarding the packages. Further, the administration may be required to make funding decisions for separate divisional units or to consolidate the separate rankings into one for a single funding. Either of these alternatives becomes a time-consuming and highly arbitrary task for top management.

Establishing a Cutoff Point

During the budget process, any organization knows it will fund some requests and not fund others. In ZBB, some packages will be funded because of their high priorities and others may or may not be funded because of their marginal priorities. Packages with high priorities deserve limited or no review, but all others should be evaluated carefully. How can the administration decide which of tens or even hundreds of packages should be analyzed closely?

The administration may establish an arbitrary cutoff point to divide packages that will receive no review or only a cursory look from those that will be studied carefully. The cutoff point may be defined in terms of absolute dollars or as a percentage of current cumulative funding related either to last year's budget or to this year's anticipated total. The cutoff will establish a division point: packages ranked above this point will receive little or no review, those below are marginal and should receive careful consideration.

The higher the cutoff percentage, the fewer packages will be subjected to careful review; therefore, the higher the management level, the more packages will be consolidated, and the higher the cutoff percentage should be. Setting the cutoff percentage at 85 percent, for example, means that packages whose cumulative funding totals less than 85 percent of last year's budget will not be reviewed closely. However, if 90 percent is the cutoff, more packages will be included in the limited or no-review group, leaving fewer for careful study.

Figure 4-2 Three Ranking Levels in a Large Hospital

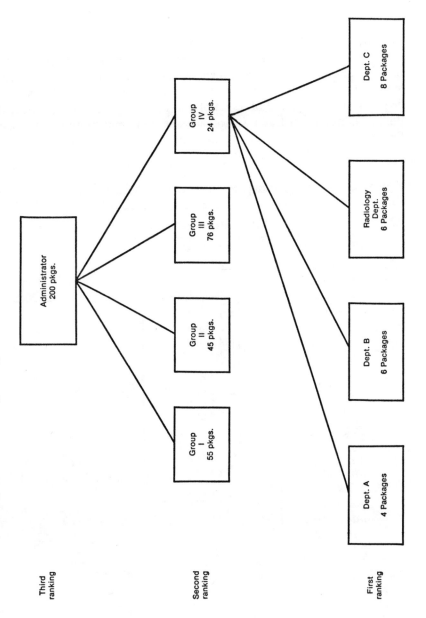

Figure 4-3 illustrates this process in a hypothetical hospital setting. It shows that at the departmental level, all decision packages are ranked in order of importance. The reranking at the supervisory level is the first opportunity for trade-offs. The supervisor must rerank all packages, and those outside the 65 percent cutoff point must be evaluated carefully as to their relative values. The assistant administrator must take the listings of the two supervisors and rerank them into a single rating. At this reranking level, the cutoff point is raised to 75 percent which requires that close review be given to packages H3 of 4, H4 of 4, RM3 of 4, and RM4 of 4. Finally, this assistant administrator and other assistant administrators will transmit their ratings to the hospital administrator for a final ranking and funding.

Figure 4-3 Decision Package Ranking Using Cutoff Points

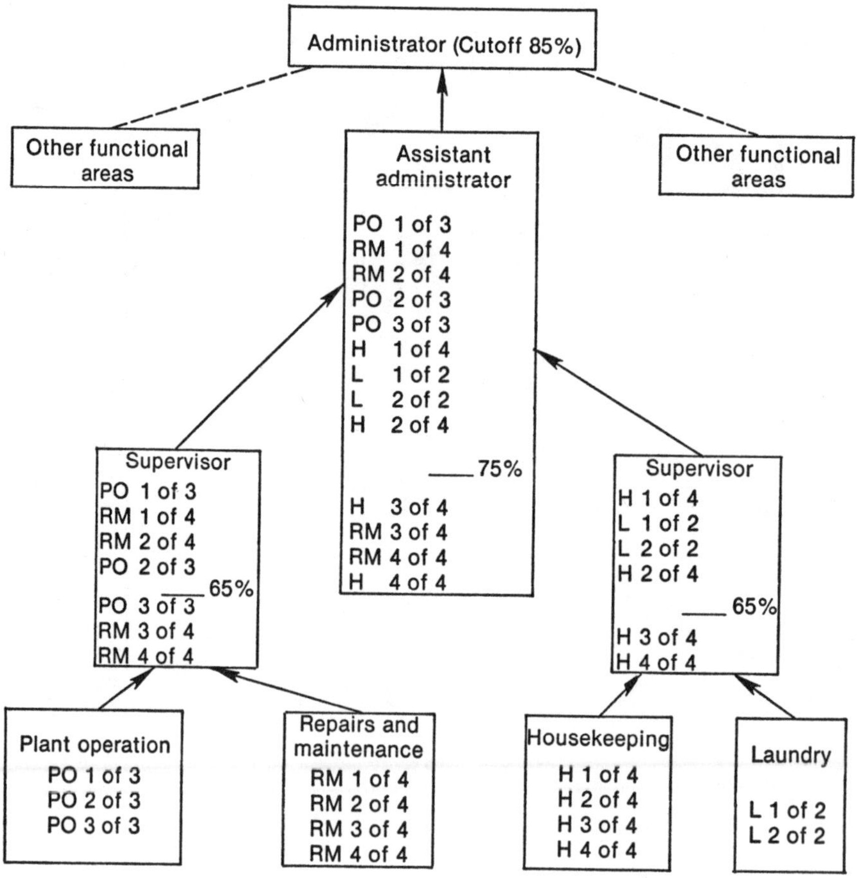

The administrator has a cutoff percentage of 85 percent, the highest in the institution.

The cutoff percentages should be established before the decision packages are prepared. The percentages are based on the cutoff level to be used by top management. The administration usually will set its cutoff at something less than 100 percent of last year's budget, say 85 percent or 90 percent. Each lower level of management will have a percentage based on the administration's. Even though package preparation should not be affected by cutoff points, some guidelines are set implicitly for minimum and normal funding. At the supervisory level in Figure 4-3, for example, packages ranked above the 65 percent cutoff are implied to be necessary while those below that point are marginal.

Package preparers and all management should be made aware that the cutoff point does not separate packages that will be funded from those that will not. Some department heads may believe the cutoff point at lowest ranking levels may be so low, say 50 percent, that packages necessary for continued operation will be left unfunded because they fall outside the percentage. The cutoff point is not a means of determining funding but of lessening the ranking problem and increasing management's efficiency when faced with large numbers of packages. All packages should be listed, even if they will not be reviewed. A complete listing gives the administration an overview of perceived priorities at lower management levels and can provide the option of varying total funding to see what packages would have to be delayed if unforeseen events restricted the availability of funds.

THE RANKING

The rankings begin at the decision unit level so unit managers may list their packages in the priority they perceive best. Rerankings can be performed (1) by an individual, as illustrated in Figure 4-3, acting alone or with input from appropriate managers or (2) by a committee of decision unit managers along with a member of the administration acting as moderator. There are advantages as well as drawbacks to each alternative.

Having a single individual rerank packages can be best if the time of decision unit managers is limited or the rating is needed quickly. The individual often can rerank projects in much less time than a committee. The individual must have a detailed knowledge of the objectives and goals of each unit and how the packages fit them. Detailed knowledge is available at lower management levels but as the reranking progresses, intimate knowledge diminishes significantly. This problem can be overcome in part through meetings at which the manager responsible for reranking collaborates with the lower level that conducted the previous ranking or another responsible individual. These meetings should be informal give-and-take discussions of the relative merits of the packages. The manager then has the sole responsibility for reranking, but the information on the packages has been supplemented with information not easily included on the package form and that may have become available since the form was prepared. Two cautionary notes before using an individualized approach to ranking:

1. The individual should be fair and objective when assessing the merits of decision packages. Although this is difficult to assure in practical situations, the individual is expected to give priority to packages that produce the greatest cost/benefit ratio to the health care institution, not those that support personal biases.
2. If an individual is using an informal committee for advice, care should be taken that undue influence is not exerted by one who has personal charisma or superb communication skills to ensure package funding. Sober and wise judgment is required of the decision maker charged with ranking. The merits of the package, not personality, must be weighed.

Another alternative is a ranking committee. A committee has the expertise necessary to evaluate numerous packages properly. Since no single person or two-person group can have a complete knowledge of each package, a committee can help solve this problem. The committee approach helps department heads see how their functional area uses and contributes to other areas. Communication and coordination between areas can be improved through the committee ranking. The committee may be composed of all department heads or, in a large facility with several organizational levels, may be made up of persons from each management level and moderated by the chief. Ranking will proceed until it reaches the top administrative level. The major drawback to the committee is the time often necessary to perform the ranking. Timely completion can be promoted if the administration establishes a time limit for the ranking.

Regardless of who makes up the ranking body—whether individual or group—the process is one of planning and decision making. The department heads have spent countless hours preparing the packages and will want a part in the decision of whether or not to fund. The administration may find itself accused of preparing the budget without giving those responsible for meeting it an adequate opportunity to provide ranking input. At some point in the process, the department head or first-line supervisor should be included in the decision.

How To Rank

There are several methods of ranking. The purpose is to obtain a list of all decision packages in the order of importance to the facility. Distinguishing the most important from the least important may not be a problem, but between the 21st and 22nd can be, particularly if only 21 packages can be funded. A further complication is the sheer number of forms to shuffle and decide upon. The cutoff point approach helps the deliberations somewhat, but if the cutoff is 60 percent of last year's budget there may remain 20 to 40 marginal packages to rank. The task is not impossible or impractical, however, if the administration is careful to establish ranking procedures and policies that are easy to apply and equitable for all. Three ranking techniques have been employed by organizations using ZBB: the voting system, the major category system, and the single criterion method.

The Voting System

This is probably the most widely used ranking system. It was used first by Texas Instruments and the state of Georgia and was developed by Peter Phyrr. It is best utilized by an organization that ranks by committee (although an individual can use the technique) and there are more than 50 packages. Some system of weighting the packages, such as one through six, with one being lowest priority, is established. As each package comes up, an overhead transparency projector may be used to show the package's details on a screen. After discussion, each member of the committee votes on a form provided for each package. Each package is considered on its overall merits. The votes are tallied and the ranking continues until an initial consensus is reached.

The initial rankings may be placed on a transparency slide and shown to the group, which then resolves any misunderstandings or inconsistencies. If, for example, two decision packages numbered B3 of 4 and B4 of 4 were ranked with B4 of 4 the higher, there may be some discussion and reranking if package B4 of 4 depends on B3 of 4's being funded. After differences are resolved, a final ranking is established for transmission to the next consolidation level. The form on which the votes are cast is illustrated in Figure 4-4. Two suggestions about the form: (1) there is no magical range of points— 1-4 could be used just as easily as 1-6, although too many points (such as 10 or more) may be confusing; and (2) whatever the range of points, all committee members must understand the voting mechanism clearly so the same standards are applied to each package.

Figure 4-4 The Voting Scale*

Decision package ____ of ____
Decision package name _____
Voter (if anonymous leave blank) _____

4	Should fund this package because of high probability of success for the organization or because it is a minimum level package.
3	Fund this package only after minimum levels are accepted.
	← Division point on accept or reject
2	Fund this package only if additional funds become available.
1	Should not fund this package because of unsure impact or for other reasons, such as spending goals.

PLACE AN *X* IN THE BLOCK YOU BELIEVE DESCRIBES YOUR VOTE ON THE DECISION PACKAGE.

Source: Zero-Base Budgeting by Peter Pyhrr. Adapted by permission of John Wiley and Sons, New York, New York, © 1972.

Major Category System

All packages are ranked based on overall merits when using the voting system just described. Clearly, some packages may have a higher priority than others simply because they fall into a certain class of items such as "legal requirements." Therefore, a variation on the voting method is to isolate each package into groups or categories. The categories have pre-determined priorities such as:

Category I—legally required
Category II—proposals that meet community health needs and have
        fast payoffs (one or two years)

Category III—proposals that meet community health needs regardless of
      payoff time
Category IV—proposals that have long-term merit and may not directly
      benefit community health immediately
Category V—all others

Each facility should establish its own categories and priorities. The administration may wish to simplify the categories by titling them: Legally Required, Most Desirable, Moderately Desirable, Less Desirable, and Not Desirable. Within each category (other than the first and, perhaps, the second) the committee should vote on the relative merits of each one vs. others in the category. The rankings would include all of Category I, Category II, and so on until funding limitations have been met.

Care must be exercised when using the major category technique. Some preparers may attempt to include normal operating costs in a package designed to meet regulatory requirements; i.e., normal personnel costs included in affirmative action proposals. Even though a package is in a legal requirements category, it should be reviewed. Preparers also may tend to overestimate the benefits of their proposal or to underestimate the costs in order to move the package up to a higher priority category. Close review and discussion in the committee meeting before voting may ferret out these problems.

Single Criterion Approach

The final ranking technique is the single criterion approach. This requires that all packages be ranked according to one element, whether it be discounted cash flow, total cash in divided by total cash out, or return on investment. Once the rankings have been established, the cutoff point is applied and projects below that point are evaluated and possibly reranked. Available funds are allocated to the packages in order of priority.

This method is quite impractical for health care institutions since most have proposals to which cash flow analyses are inappropriate. It may be of value when ranking capital project packages but can result in some worthless rankings if used wholesale. For example, assume that a nursing home's management was faced with ranking several packages, one of which required it to modify its hallways to meet requirements of the Occupational Safety and Health Administration. If this package were ranked on a cash flow basis, the result would be a low ranking, no funding, and a violation of legal requirements. Other equally important projects could be ranked low, based on a single criterion, and remain postponed or unfunded.

Chapter 5

Answers to Commonly Asked Questions About Zero-Base Budgeting

The administration of any health care facility generally will have specific questions that have not been answered in the previous chapters. This chapter presents answers to the more common ones that apply to most health care organizations contemplating the use of zero-base budgeting.

If my hospital has no formalized budget procedures, should we even consider zero-base budgeting?

Zero-base budgeting does not rely on previous budgeting systems for its success. Zero-base is a tool for making planning decisions and may be used whether or not budgeting systems preceded it. The major advantage to having a predecessor system is that department heads or clinician-managers may be accustomed to being involved in the planning and programming decision process. This is not true, however, if an authoritative budget process was used, with the administration dictating departmental spending levels. The major disadvantage to having a predecessor system is the possibility that there will be a resistance to changing from the familiar system to ZBB. Even shifting from a participative system to ZBB involves change and possibly some resistance. Both problems can be avoided in part by the administration's commitment to ZBB and selling its benefits to those charged with developing the basic information.

How do we know whether zero-base budgeting is applicable to our institution and whether we should use it?

Zero-base budgeting is applicable to any organization that has discretionary or managed costs. Actually, that could be broadened to say that ZBB pertains mainly, but not exclusively, to "staff" costs. In a hospital setting, for example, staff costs would include administration, patient accounts, patient records, maintenance, housekeeping, data processing, laundry, and all areas that must use subjective cost/benefit measures.

Zero-base budgeting may be applied to revenue-generating departments that consistently have been allotted incremental resources justified by expected corresponding revenue increases. The decision package would identify the additional revenues to be generated by the additional cost and could be used to determine whether the department head's expectations were greater than the potential achievements. Under incremental budgeting, department heads often are not questioned about their expenditures if additional revenues are expected to exceed the additional costs. The hospital pharmacy, for example, may request one additional employee who will be expected to earn at least one and a half times the annual salary in increased revenues. At the end of the year, or earlier if possible, the department head can evaluate whether this objective is being or has been achieved. If decision packages are required for revenue-generating departments, the department head must be more concerned with the accuracy of the predictions in the package.

The second half of the question is somewhat more difficult to answer. Authorities have said ZBB is for large companies. The federal government, the state of Georgia, and Westinghouse are large organizations that use ZBB. Most of the organizations reported in the news media as ZBB adopters are in Fortune's largest 1,000 companies.

Whether a particular institution should use ZBB should be answered by evaluating the present planning and decision-making process. If the present system does not provide adequate information so that the administration knows what it is getting for its costs, ZBB may be appropriate. If clinician-managers or department heads are preparing their budgets by taking last year's costs plus an increment for the current year with no thought to expected results or effects, ZBB may be appropriate. If the administration is faced with budget cuts and does not wish to make equal across-the-board reductions, ZBB will provide a means to reduce expenditures in areas of least benefit. ZBB is *not* for the health care facility with an administration that is not totally committed to implementing the system and becoming involved in its successful operation.

Will zero-base budgeting reduce our total costs or simply reallocate existing funds within the organization?

The answer could be: either, neither, or both. First, it must be understood that ZBB does not do anything of itself; the people who use it affect the organization's costs. ZBB is simply a management tool that assists in the decision process. Some have contended that the use of ZBB in the federal government would reduce costs to taxpayers. Others have said ZBB would help release funds from programs of low benefit to be channeled to programs of greater benefit. According to the federal government's budget estimates for fiscal year 1979 (the first year of ZBB in the executive branch), no significant reduction appears to be forthcoming. Reallocations of funds between agencies or programs are subtle, if they exist at all. There are political considerations, including legislative figures with political mini-kingdoms, that may not be changed in the short run by ZBB. Nevertheless, many more bureaucrats now have a better grasp of their functional area's programs because of the ZBB process.

ZBB was designed to show where costs could be cut, not how to cut. The technique grew out of a need to reduce total expenditures at Texas Instruments by eliminating the least beneficial spending. Therefore, ZBB was used initially to reallocate costs to more beneficial elements. In the state of Georgia, however, there was disagreement over whether reallocations within state agencies actually occurred. (See pages 121–138: "A Look at Zero-Base Budgeting—The Georgia Experience.")

Positive cost savings have been reported by the Southern California Edison Company ($300,000 per year), Westinghouse's turbine division ($4.2 million), and the Bank of Montreal (6 percent of head office expenses), all claiming ZBB as the cause. Clearly, the answer could be either, neither, or both, depending on who is answering the question. A well designed and well implemented ZBB system can reduce and reallocate expenditures, but only if the people using the system wish to do so.

Are there characteristics of functional areas that should be prime candidates for cost savings that may be isolated by the zero-base budgeting process?

There are four areas that may prove fruitful for isolating cost savings:

1. departments that provide services similar to those offered by other departments
2. departments with long-tenured managers
3. departments with new managers
4. departments that have had some recent innovation, additional program, or other change

One of the purposes of using zero-base budgeting is to determine whether any services are being duplicated. Since each department manager must disclose the utilization of resources allocated to that department, all of that unit's activities are presented in decision packages submitted by the manager. Department reports to the individual responsible for oversight of these units may disclose activities that are performed by two or more areas. Overlapping or duplicated activities may be found, for example, in services provided by the housekeeping and grounds and maintenance departments.

Departments with managers who have been with the organization for either a long or a short time may be sources of cost efficiencies for completely different reasons. Close scrutiny of decision packages submitted by long-tenured department heads may reveal efficiencies due to domains built over a period of years through incremental budgeting. The departmental budget may have grown by continuous annual increases atop the base available when the manager was appointed. On the other hand, cost efficiencies may be isolated where the department head is new. The new head may be less threatened by admitting that certain programs and resources are unneeded because they were installed by a predecessor.

Departments with recent program changes or innovations may have had resources that were found unneeded even though they were expected to be used when the project was justified originally. For example, a project that initially required two full-time equivalent employees may require only one now. However, the department head may be somewhat reluctant to release the additional staff person if there is no pressure to do so. Sometimes innovative techniques, such as consolidation of activities, may have been justified by the expectation of a reduction of one FTE when in fact two FTE's could be eliminated or reassigned.

Everyone in our hospital understands and makes annual input to our present incremental budgeting system and it seems to work fine. Why should we replace it with zero-base?

Zero-base budgeting does not have to supplant the present budget system in its entirety. It can be used for some areas of the institution and not for others; for example, all staff or support areas may use zero-base budgeting while revenue producers may not.

Most private companies have used zero-base budgeting as a supplement to traditional budgeting or for specific departments only. Texas Instruments, the first major corporation to use ZBB, adopted the technique in a few staff level departments. Xerox later used zero-base budgeting, but the several dozen department heads applying the technique also were using traditional budgeting and supplementing their requests with information generated through zero-base decision packages. There are several cases where an entire organization converted to zero-base budgeting even though a more traditional system had been used for years. The state of Georgia and the executive branch of the federal government are notable examples of wholesale conversion.

Is is hard work to replace, albeit partially, something old and comfortable with something new and different. It should be pointed out that many organizations have made the same decision. Some counted the costs and said, "No, we won't change." Perhaps a checklist will assist in making a decision for or against zero-base budgeting. Can you answer *Yes* to each of the following?

- Every one of our programs or activities is essential to the institution or the community's health care.
- All of our programs or activities are of equal importance.
- All of our programs or activities should be continued on the same timetable and at the present level of effort.
- No alternatives exist for the present methods used to perform our programs or activities that may reduce effort or cost.
- All activities and programs, since they are of equal importance and essential to the institution, should be funded at last year's level plus a percentage, with no further justification necessary.

It would be comforting to answer all those statements positively; however, not many objective administrators can do that. Zero-base budgeting will not change the negative answers to positive, but it will provide more and better information so the administration knows both what is happening and what is not.

Doesn't the paperwork increase over traditional budgeting make zero-base budgeting ineffectual?

It must be remembered that paperwork increases are measured against some existing quantity. Paperwork will increase under zero-base budgeting if previous decisions were made subjectively without written justifications based on objectives and goals. The added paperwork may be beneficial in these cases because plans are written, evaluation criteria established, alternatives examined, and costs estimated that result in a more informed funding decision. In some instances, paperwork may decrease relative to the existing system. The reduction may occur where budget preparers have been using a multiplicity of forms and systems that have evolved over time in each department. ZBB will result in a single system and a homogeneous set of forms that will replace the many. Moreover, in years after the zero-base system is installed, organizations have noted a decrease in paperwork as management became more familiar with the methods and procedures. "Horror" stories tell of organizations that used zero-base budgeting being swamped with paperwork. *Business Week* in April 1977 referred to a Navy experiment in ZBB that increased the budget documentation from 150 pages to 2,000 pages. Isolated examples of massive increases in paper should not stop an administrator or health care facility manager from using zero-base budgeting.

The first year of implementation may see more paperwork, but huge increases can be averted by careful planning. Policies may be established whereby:

1. decision packages are limited to one page, front and back
2. decision packages must be prepared for dollar sums of a specified minimum amount or greater or if 1 FTE is being considered
3. decision packages must be prepared by personnel no lower in the organization chart than department chief or manager

A paperwork increase may be limited by following the advice of one budget manager who proposed an informal approach in which the budget director discusses the requests ranging from minimum funding to spending for new services with the cost center manager.

I've heard that zero-base budgeting is a dynamic process. What is meant by that?

The completed zero-base budget provides a set of financial plans based on organizational objectives and goals. It forms a static plan for a changing institution, not unlike a traditionally prepared budget. When ZBB becomes operational as the fiscal year begins, there is a significant departure from the traditional budget. The zero-base budget separates important activities from marginal ones through the ranking process. Therefore, if funds are reduced or revenue estimates are not meeting expectations, activities that were ranked low but accepted for funding may be delayed or omitted until financial conditions improve. Department chiefs often will be more receptive to budget cuts if they realize the activities being omitted or delayed were marginal to begin with and would have been accepted only if funds should meet expected levels. Clearly, this is better than across-the-board cuts. On the other hand, if additional funds become available, through grants or endowments, for example, projects left unfunded have been ranked already and can be evaluated once more, along with any package proposals developed subsequent to the budget's preparation, and funds may be allocated to the most beneficial ones.

It should not be forgotten that decision package preparation is not relegated to a once-a-year exercise. Any time an idea or a requirement for a new activity arises, a package may be prepared and submitted for consideration if funds become available. Even if the package is not funded during the year, the information need only be updated for submission as a part of the next year's budget.

We have budget games played in our present system. Are there budget games we may encounter in a zero-base system and what can the administration do to avoid them?

Two possible budget games may occur in an organization using ZBB: (1) ranking pet projects of higher management low and (2) "holing up" until the zero-base fad is over. The first problem was reported in the state of Georgia in ZBB's initial phases. Managers would rank their own personally desirable projects high while rating those known to be favored by upper management low. In this way, the manager was wagering that top management would extend funding to the lower ranked projects because of its personal biases, and the manager's projects also would be funded because of the high ranking. The best solution is an informed, careful review by the administration. All packages should be listed so priorities may be questioned and, if challenges are valid, can be reranked.

The other problem occurs when established department chiefs or managers perceive that zero-base budgeting is a fad and, like a common headache, will pass. In this situation, some department managers will prepare decision packages with a careless attitude, resulting in incomplete or incomprehensible forms. The solution, of course, is to give department heads an original perception of the administration's complete commitment to the concept of zero-base budgeting. All administrative memoranda and correspondence regarding ZBB must persuade all levels of management toward commitment and involvement. Sometimes poorly prepared decision packages resulting from a lack of interest will require the administration to insist that they be revised one or more times if they do not come up to reasonable expectations. If the administration is not committed to seeing the best results from these efforts, the outcome will be a mediocrity or, worse, a failure.

Another game package preparers may play could involve the use of "hype" words in the justification for the expenditure, expecting that the person ranking the packages would be encouraged, or even frightened, into rating that unit as a higher priority item. Phrases such as "reduction of quality control," "increase disease communication," and "reducing overall quality of work" may be used in the decision package in an effort to inspire higher rankings. Management can do little to avoid the occurrence of these phrases except to require that when a qualitative phrase is used, some quantitative measure be applied so the potential effect can be determined.

Why not start a pilot program and see if it works for us, then install the entire zero-base budgeting system?

Pilot programs often are doomed to failure just because they are pilot programs. They lack a sense of permanence in that most people view such an approach as a problem-finding venture. If the problems found are too many or too great, the program will be abandoned. Those who resist the change tend to provide enough problems or potential problems so the administration will become frustrated and retreat to the old ways. This book was written to help administrators preview potential difficulties and prepare for them. A pilot program should not be necessary if administrators do their homework and prepare a secure infrastructure of guidelines, procedures, forms, and education before the system becomes operational. To be sure, the zero-based system will evolve over the years as new information peculiar to the organization emerges. The initial zero-base system may not resemble completely the operation five years hence.

Must we employ zero-base budgeting throughout the organization or can we select departments to use it?

Many companies have used zero-based budgeting in only part of the organization. There are limitations and problems in this approach. One problem is behavioral, in that the departments or subunits selected for a zero-base budgeting model may feel discriminated against because they believe it will take additional time and effort. This problem can be overcome by stressing the benefits ZBB will provide to the department's decision-making abilities.

Another problem is operational: how should the zero-base process function? The people responsible for ranking the decision packages must have all packages available to them so they can make trade-offs between departments. When some departments submit decision packages and other departments are not required to, the decision maker does not have all of the necessary information available. This was a very real problem for the Alexian Brothers Medical Center (Appendix B) when it realized that a decision package could be ranked at the lowest priority within a department but that low-ranked packages could be more important in terms of meeting institutional goals than the highest-ranked package of another department that was not under the zero-base concept. Therefore, if all departments are not under the zero-base methodology, a complete, effective ranking of all organizational activities represented by decision packages cannot take place.

In a health care organization, who is the appropriate person to initiate the zero-base process once it has been decided such a process is appropriate?

It may be advisable to have the person in charge of operational matters, whether it be the administrator or assistant administrator for operations, to send out the memorandum initiating the process and advising on the steps to take. It may be inappropriate for the controller or another financial officer to begin the process because the hospital staff, management, and department heads may perceive that undue emphasis is being placed on profitability or other financial matters to the detriment of quality health care.

Are there any problems we can expect even if we have a well-thought-out operational plan for our zero-base system?

There always will be problems in any new system. William W. Phelps, manager, budgets and financial planning for the Power Systems Group of Combustion Engineering, Inc., has developed a list of 15 considerations to make before embarking on a zero-base program. His "Phelps Fifteen" follows this chapter and may be helpful in avoiding problems before they occur.

Readings

ZERO-BASE BUDGETING:
PRACTICAL IMPLEMENTATION*

During the past few years, and in particular, in recent months, there has been a great deal of interest in the zero-base budgeting technique. This interest has stemmed largely from publicity received from applications at Texas Instruments and in the State of Georgia. Since these initial efforts, a number of companies including service organizations, governmental units including state, town and municipalities as well as school districts have implemented zero-base programs.

Along with the growing interest in zero-base budgeting, there has also been increasingly a number of articles published on the subject. Since Peter Phyrr's book,[1] many articles have appeared in various newspapers and financial journals. However, most of these have tended to relay to the reader the mechanics of ZBB and little has been written about the day-to-day problems usually encountered in the development and implementation of such a program.

The purpose of this article, therefore, is not to discuss mechanics but to offer some observations concerning development and implementation. Each individual application takes on its own character and, in many instances, reflects the particular organization and management team. However, for those who are about to embark upon a ZBB program, these observations may be of some benefit.

---

*Reprinted from *Managerial Planning* by William W. Phelps by permission of Planning Executives Institute, Oxford, Ohio, © July-August, 1977.

---

[1] Peter A. Pyhrr. *Zero-Base Budgeting: A Practical Management Tool for Evaluating Expenses* (New York: John Wiley & Sons, 1973).

Phelps' Fifteen

One ... Obtain Senior Management Endorsement, Cooperation and Participation

In most organizations, the zero-base budgeting technique usually is born in either one of two ways. First, the chief executive has read something about it, thinks it is a good idea and "sells" it to his budget director. The second way, and usually most often, the budget director "sells" the chief executive. In either case, all the work and long hours spent in developing a program for the organization will be to no avail and, perhaps, the program doomed for failure if the chief executive is not out front during the entire process. Merely endorsing the program is not enough. After a program has been developed and the "kick-off" meetings have been held, his total cooperation and participation is necessary. There are numerous difficulties during implementation without the CEO being one of them. He must demonstrate to all levels of management that this is a serious undertaking and it is what HE wants and not merely the whims of the budget director. In order for the process to work, the CEO must participate in all phases of the program. His presence and actions during implementation sessions, development of decision packages and ranking forms and the review process will largely determine the success of the program.

Two ... Goals—Set Them and Get To Them

At the outset and very importantly so, senior management must communicate to all levels of management the approved goals and objectives developed by the organization. This may be simply the management by objectives (M.B.O.) approach or, more sophisticated, in the form of a formalized strategic planning process. Without the transmittal of goals and objectives, the people responsible for the preparation of the decision packages at the lower management levels will not know the direction of the organization. It must be recognized that these are the same individuals who are responsible for the running of the business on an everyday basis. Also, the goals and objectives should be specific in content so that there is no question as to what is intended for the organization. Generalities will result in decision packages that will not give the chief executive viable alternatives and the mechanism to reduce operating expenses effectively; and, perhaps more important, defeat the purpose of zero-base budgeting.

Three ... Before Starting—Review Organization

Is your organization ready for zero-base budgeting? Is it the type of organization, in part or whole, that is conducive to zero-base budgeting? Many organizations have had a very successful budget program for many years using what has been labeled the "incremental approach." This approach assumes that the activities previously funded are cost efficient and must be perpetuated. Depending on the chief executive and the emphasis he has placed on budgeting, abandonment of a successful program for zero-base budgeting may not be in the best interests of the company. Remember, there are some companies that have tried ZBB and have had little success. There may be many reasons why they failed, but the fact remains that some have. If you determine that zero-base budgeting is really for you, take the necessary time before you implement a broad base program to review the organization. There may be operations within the company that zero-budgeting does not apply to. As stated in the literature, direct manufacturing operations are usually excluded from the effort. But what about other departments where it may not be as obvious? The engineering department, the drafting department and field construction activities are just a few that should be reviewed before you start. In many companies, these types of activities are directly related to contract backlog and the work load in these departments is dictated by delivery dates, schedules, etc. To zero-base these activities tends to be an exercise. However, this does not mean that these "exempted" departments are exempt from budgeting. Cost center managers must still justify staffing and related operating expenses. Zero-base budgeting is really intended for staff type organizations or departments and this is where the best results of your zero-base efforts will be.

Four ... Obtain Adequate Staff

This may appear to be heresy. How can a budget director who is responsible for implementing a zero-base budgeting program request additional staffing at the outset? Your budget department may be adequately staffed. Usually, this is not the case. It must be noted that the ZBB concept does not eliminate the work load and budget systems currently in existence. The ZBB concept is a means to an end, a substitute for compiling and justifying an operating expense budget. Once the ZBB technique has been used to prepare the budget, detailed budgets for each cost center by type of expense is usually required, budgeting programs are still maintained, etc. Because nothing is really eliminated from the work load of the budget department, new staffing may be required to handle the new activities brought about by zero-base budgeting. In order for you to have a successful program, there has to be constant support from the budget department during the development of the decision packages as well as review by all levels of management. One of the most important aspects of any zero-base program is feedback. It is imperative that the people who prepared the detailed decision packages and ranking forms be evaluated and inconsistencies, deficiencies, etc., be discussed and corrected. If not, the same quality of product will be apparent the next time and little will be gained toward accomplishing a successful program. A little expenditure at the outset will go a long way in the future.

Five ... Set Up Local Contacts

Regardless of the size of the organization, it is necessary for each functional group to designate a zero-base budget coordinator. This individual should be thoroughly familiar with that area, i.e., its function, activities, budgeting process, etc. In order to have an effective program, it will be necessary to interface with the members of the budget department. It will ease the whole process if all concerned know where to go to get questions answered, consultations for difficulties encountered, as well as designating an individual who will be responsible for ensuring the program is being completed on schedule and properly.

Six ... Establish Review Procedures

All the best intended programs will fail if an adequate review procedure has not been established. All the time and effort to develop viable decision packages and ranking forms by priority will mean little or nothing if not adequately reviewed. A review procedure must be established for all levels of management prior to the zero-base data being submitted to the budget department. This critical review at the lowest level of management to the highest will ensure that the budget data submitted meets the requirements established for the organization and that only those activities that are necessary and cost efficient will be perpetuated if approved by the chief executive.

But what about after the data reaches the budget department and is reviewed, consolidated and summarized, etc.? What type of review is to be held by the chief executive? How much of the detail will he have to review? What decisions will be necessary if the overall budget submitted does not meet his profitability goals? One of the most effective ways to accomplish a top management review is for the chief executive to establish a ZBB review committee. This committee might consist of some of the senior management who report directly to him. The scrutiny of peers, especially where line and staff have equal voice, will add much to ensure that adequate review has taken place. The budget committee then makes a recommendation to the CEO as to the budget funding level. Of course, final levels will still be the responsibility of the CEO. Those in senior management who feel that budget committee decisions are detrimental to their particular organization, can recommend trade-offs and establish new priorities. But regardless of the type of review or steps involved, a formal review process should be established and incorporated in the organization's zero-base budgeting manual.

Seven ... Important—Get Off to a Good Start

While other aspects of the program may be as equally important, the initial efforts, if properly administered, will enhance the effort. There are many things that contribute to the success of a program. First of all, the "kick-off" or the announcement by the chief executive, usually in the form of a letter to his staff, will set the tone and general atmosphere concerning the ZBB. Here the chief executive must state that the program has his endorsement as well as what he expects from such an undertaking.

Once this has been done, it is now up to the budget people to develop and implement it on a professional basis. The development and printing of a ZBB manual should be done on a "best effort" basis. Also, the decision package form as well as the ranking form should be professionally developed, perhaps by a graphics consultant. These forms should contain only essential information such as description, consequences if eliminated, alternatives and cost and resource analyses. It should be a workable format.

Once the forms and manual have been published and distributed to the cost center managers and other levels of management, introductory training sessions should be held. Small groups of individuals who will be developing the decision packages should attend. This provides the opportunity for the budget director to describe the zero-base concept, as well as to explain how the program is being implemented throughout the organization. It also presents the opportunity for a question and answer period before actual work is started. The more sessions held with small groups, the broader the coverage.

A very important part of any program is the trial period. A limited scope application, perhaps with a few staff groups, will help determine if there are any problem areas or "soft spots" in your program. It also gives the budget director an opportunity to evaluate the manual, forms, implementation process as well as the concept itself. It will also point out deficiencies in the program as well as whether there is adequate staffing in the budget area to handle a broader application.

Eight ... Re-evaluate Program After Trial Period

All during the development of a ZBB effort, many questions will arise and difficulties will be encountered. Most of these will be solved as experience is gained by the budget staff as well as by the people developing the decision packages. However, once you become involved in such a program, it is often times difficult to step back and objectively evaluate what has transpired to date. But, it must be done! Remember, a lot of effort has gone into the ZBB program up to this point. But it has been rather limited in relation to implementation throughout the entire organization. Again, these questions must be asked and answered: Does the concept apply to the organization? Are there any areas that should be exempted? Did the trial period give the results intended? Is this a better way to develop a budget as compared to the traditional approach? Other areas to consider include senior management participation, the reaction of the cost center managers, the quality of their accomplishments, and the zero-budget staff. Many areas should be critically evaluated before embarking on a total commitment.

Nine ... Beware of the "Experts"

No matter what organization, there will always be the so-called experts. These are the people who claim that they have been doing zero-budgeting, project budgeting, manpower planning or whatever for years and cannot see the relevancy of the "new program." And also, there will be those who feel that they have a better way as to how the program should work, usually to their best interests. However, not all comments should be discounted. Many may see things that have been overlooked and these observations may improve the program.

Ten ... Expect to Spend a Lot of Time

A zero-base budgeting program regardless of the organization will require the time and effort of many people. It must be recognized that management, i.e., all levels from the front-line supervisor to the chief executive, must be involved in the process. The supervisors and cost center managers are usually responsible for determining the activities that provide the basis of the decision packages and must establish priorities by ranking the decision packages. This is a very time consuming effort—especially the first time through. Once this has been accomplished, successive levels of management must then review the zero-base information, changing priorities if necessary and consolidating cost centers under their operational control.

Budget reviews by senior management, whether by executive committee or by the chief executive, must be held. From this activity, final priorities and funding levels will be established. This total commitment of management resources is necessary for successful implementation. This must be understood by all at the outset.

Eleven . . . Beware of the Paperwork Generated

One of the advantages of zero-base budgeting is that all activities of the organization will be thoroughly documented. This perhaps is also a disadvantage in that many decision packages and ranking forms will be prepared. The question arises: What do you do with it all? If done properly, the amount of paperwork can be minimized if cost center managers realistically develop decision packages giving management viable alternatives. To prepare decision packages detailing activities to tenths of people, especially in a small cost center performing a singular function is not necessary and should be avoided. Proper structuring of cost center activities will eliminate many unnecessary decision packages. Another reason for a large volume of decision packages is "manager defensiveness." This occurs when a manager tries to "beat the system" by reducing activities to unpractical levels so as to prohibit actual budget reductions.

Another way to effectively manage the amount of paper generated, assuming that measures have been taken as outlined above, is to computerize the decision packages. By taking selected information from the decision package, a properly executed program will summarize levels, costs and staffing. This will facilitate the review process at higher management levels. Of course, the detailed decision packages with the attendant justification will be available for detailed review if necessary.

Twelve . . . Maintain Contacts

Once the zero-base program is underway and cost center managers are in the process of developing decision packages, contact should be maintained with the various zero-base coordinators. Many questions concerning mechanics, the structuring of decision packages, recognizing activities as well as levels within activities can be answered before decision packages are completed and submitted for review and approval. In most organizations, zero-base budgeting is a traumatic experience for the cost center manager who must now justify his existence. By maintaining contact, difficulties with the process will be minimized.

Thirteen ... Important! Follow-Up Activities

A zero-base program once implemented is a continuous effort. Vital to the success of initial efforts as well as to future efforts is the amount of feedback. It must be demonstrated that something was done to the material generated. This is not always easy. Given limitations of time during the budget season and perhaps a deficiency in obtaining adequate staffing, feedback still must be given to the people who prepared the decision packages. Obviously, the preferred way would be to have the budget director sit down with each cost center manager and critique his efforts. Across the table dialogue is extremely beneficial and deficiencies could be corrected. However, this is a very time consuming process. Every effort should be made to do this, even if spaced out over a period of time. An immediate remedy is to prepare an appraisal checklist noting major deficiencies in the preparation of decision packages and ranking forms that require attention. In this way, immediate feedback is given to the cost center manager. Then when time allows, the detailed critique meetings can be held.

Fourteen ... Do Not Expect an Immediate R.O.I.

Like any new undertaking, there will be mixed results. Depending on personalities and the emphasis placed at various management levels of the organization, (it must be recognized that due to differences in management styles, results within the same organization will differ), information received in the form of decision packages and priority ranking forms will vary. Some will be above average and some will be less than adequate. Usually, results will follow the normal distribution along the bell-shaped curve. Improvements in the future will be a direct result of the personal contacts established, if not already done, maintaining contacts as well as, and most important, conducting feedback activities.

There will also be a number of areas, such as, formats, schedules, review activities and feedback activities which will require review after the completion of the initial effort. Familiar words such as, "we should have" will be evident. These areas will be the ones where changes will take place the next time zero budgeting is used to prepare an operating expense budget.

To reap the benefits of zero-base budgeting, the technique must be applied over a period of time, perhaps three or four years. It takes more than one application to realize the proposed benefits. Also, consistently applied, modifying where necessary, there will be advantages to the organization for some time to come. There may also be benefits which were not thought of at the outset.

Fifteen ... Do Not Expect Miracles!

As with number "FOURTEEN," do not expect everything to be perfect the first time through. The message here is not to become discouraged. It will be necessary to maintain a positive attitude in order that modifications can be implemented and carried out. Also, senior management may want an assessment of the initial effort. While there may be deficiencies, and they certainly should be pointed out, positive factors should also be noted.

Conclusion

While many aspects of zero-base budgeting are not new to the budgeting process, the implementation of a formalized technique can and will have broad ramifications throughout the organization. Therefore, it will be necessary to present the process in a well organized and thought out manner.

The "PHELPS' FIFTEEN" outlined above are concerned with the development of a zero-base budgeting program and the implementation process. While all fifteen areas require attention, in varying degrees, the success of a program rests with the participation of the chief executive officer and the support by other senior management. Careful attention should also be given to the preparation of the zero-budget manual, the introductory training sessions, the trial period, the review process, and to follow-up activities.

The benefits of a well planned zero-base effort, although usually not realized immediately, will be reaped over a period of time. Activities that are vital to the organization will be properly funded. Marginal or questionable activities will be scrutinized. Budget reductions will be made using documented information. Arbitrary budget reductions will be avoided. However, like most new endeavors, problems will be encountered. If some of the observations outlined above are considered, perhaps difficulties will be kept to a minimum.

A LOOK AT ZERO-BASE BUDGETING—
THE GEORGIA EXPERIENCE*

Former Governor Jimmy Carter introduced zero-base budgeting in the state government of Georgia. Other states are now following this example. Possibly the federal government will also implement this method in its various agencies.

In November 1970 Jimmy Carter was elected governor of the state of Georgia. Mr. Carter had campaigned on the central issue of reorganization of the Executive Branch of Georgia's government, and he began making plans for reorganization immediately after being elected. During his research, he discovered an article by Peter Phyrr in the November-December 1970 issue of the *Harvard Business Review* describing the zero-base budgeting system implemented by Texas Instruments, Inc.[1] His interest in this subject caused him to invite Mr. Phyrr to Atlanta in February 1971 to discuss the feasibility of installing this system in the state government of Georgia.

As a result of this meeting between Governor Carter and Mr. Phyrr, the decision was reached to implement zero-base budgeting in the state government of Georgia for the fiscal year 1972–1973. Mr. Phyrr was offered and accepted a temporary position as consultant to the Bureau of the Budget.

On January 11, 1972, Governor Carter introduced the new zero-base budgeting system in his State of the State Address to the General Assembly of Georgia.[2] In doing so, he stated: "It gives us a unique zero-base budgeting procedure which is almost certain to be copied throughout the Nation."[3]

In his Budget Address to the Joint Session of the General Assembly of Georgia on January 13, 1972, Governor Carter credited the early implementation of his reorganization study and the new zero-base budget for cutting the spending plans for the current year by $55 million.[4] He further reported that these cuts were made with no significant decrease in state services. In referring to zero-base budgeting, Governor Carter made the following remarks:

"Zero-base budgeting requires every agency in state government to identify each function it performs and the personnel and cost to the taxpayers for performing that function. ...

"The intense analysis which goes into the construction of a decision

* Reprinted from *The Atlanta Economic Review* by George S. Minmier and Roger H. Hermanson by permission of Georgia State University, © July–August 1976.

package begins at a low level of management within an agency. Constant review and refinement take place at each succeeding level. Each agency assigns a priority to all of its decision packages, and this information is utilized in the allocation of funds in the budget. ...

"By requiring department heads and their subordinates to take a close look at what they could do with *less* money, zero-base budgeting encourages the search for more efficient ways to do the job.

"By requiring clear descriptions of the results to be expected from every dollar spent, zero-base budgeting makes it possible to evaluate the performance of an agency against its budget. ...

"As a result of these techniques we have a budget based on cost analysis and priority ranking. We have a budget in which justification for every dollar was required—for old programs as well as new."[5]

Prior to the change to the zero-base budgeting system, Georgia had used an incremental budgeting system. The basic difference between these systems is that under the incremental approach the prior year's budget is the starting point in developing the next year's budget, but under the zero-base system the planners start from "zero." This means that merely because an item was included in last year's budget does not mean it will appear in the budget for the following year.

Incremental Budgeting. Incremental budgeting is an extension of the theory of incrementalism, which refers to making changes in small bits or increments. As applied to budgeting, incrementalism suggests that attention be directed toward the changes or marginal differences that occur between existing appropriations and proposed expenditures.[6] Such a process accepts the existing base and examines only the increments which extend the current budgeting program into the future. This procedure causes the curve of government activities to be continuous with few zigzags or breaks.

Incremental analysis is an extension of the theory of incremental budgeting. It was developed by Charles E. Lindblom. Under this approach, the task of deciding is simplified in a number of ways. Rather than being concerned with everything, the decision maker deals with:

1. only that limited set of policy alternatives that are politically relevant, those typically being policies only incrementally different from existing policies;
2. analysis of only those aspects of policies with respect to which the alternatives differ;
3. a view of the policy choice or one in a succession of choices;
4. the marginal values of various social objectives and constraints;
5. an intermixture of evaluation and empirical analysis rather than an

empirical analysis of the consequences of policies for objectives independently determined; and
6. only a small number out of all the important relevant values.[7]

Zero-Base Budgeting. In this study the term "zero-base budgeting" refers to a highly structured and systematic budgeting system as developed by Texas Instruments, Inc., and as applied in the state of Georgia 1972–1973 fiscal year's budget. Within this context, zero-base budgeting is defined as:

"An operating, planning and budgeting process which requires each manager to justify his entire budget request in detail, and shifts the burden of proof to each manager to justify why he should spend any money. This procedure requires that all activities and operations be identified in decision packages which will be evaluated and ranked in order of importance by systematic analysis."[8]

The predominant theory of budgeting applied now, as in the past, is some form of incremental budgeting. It is significant to note that in recent years there have been indications that many administrators are becoming dissatisfied with this traditional theory of incremental budgeting, as evidenced by their recommendations to change to a zero-base approach in solving budget allocation problems. In a 1961 appearance before a United States Subcommittee, Maurice Stans, Budget Director under President Eisenhower, stated: "Every item in a budget ought to be on trial for its life each year and matched against all the other claimants to our resources."[9]

Zero-base budgeting is especially adaptable to discretionary cost areas in which service and support are the primary outputs. It is this characteristic of zero-base budgeting that has attracted the interest of governmental officials, as most expenditures of government can be classified as discretionary in nature.

Methodology

To determine the degree of success of the change in the budgeting system used in Georgia an empirical study was made. The following steps were taken in the investigation:

1. Preliminary interviews were held with selected departmental budget analysts to identify topic areas for inclusion in a questionnaire.
2. A questionnaire was prepared and distributed to all 39 budgeting analysts who were using the zero-base system.

3. Follow-up interviews were conducted with selected departmental budget analysts based on their responses to the questionnaire.
4. Interviews were held with selected department heads and with former Governor Jimmy Carter.
5. A detailed examination was made of the zero-base budgeting procedures presently employed.
6. The executive budgets for the state of Georgia were reviewed for the fiscal year 1972, 1973, and 1974.

Of the 39 questionnaires, 32 were returned—a response rate of 82 percent.

For convenience in examining the acceptability or unacceptability of the zero-base budgeting system, two levels of management are distinguished: top management and middle management. Top management consists of the governor and department heads. Middle management consists of budgeting personnel at lower organizational levels within the departments. In addition to the two levels of management mentioned, the attitudes of the budget analysts in the Department of Planning and Budget concerning the zero-based budgeting system were sought.

The Office of Planning and Budget (OPB) is the staff department charged with the responsibility of ensuring that departments comply with the state's budget directives. In addition, staff budget analysts assist the departments with their budget preparation.

Top Management's Reactions

The zero-base budgeting system had the full support of Governor Carter. This is evidenced by his statement in an interview conducted on January 7, 1974: "I think our zero-base budgeting system is great for management's decision-making.... Zero-base budgeting, in itself, has given me an extremely valuable method by which I can understand what happens deep in a department." [10]

Mr. Carter also was very pleased with the ability of the zero-base budgeting system to provide relevant management information, stating that in his opinion the new budget system's greatest contribution had been in the area of improved management information. An example of the contribution of zero-base budgeting in this area was given by Mr. Carter during the interview. He stated:

"Because of zero-base budgeting we were able to determine that seven different agencies had the responsibility for the education of deaf children. When we broke down the 11,000 or so decision packages and put a computer number on each kind of function, those functions were very quickly identified as being duplicated." [11]

However, Mr. Carter's strong support of the zero-base budgeting system was not shared by some of the department heads. Of 13 department heads interviewed during this survey, only 2 indicated strong support for the zero-base budgeting system. The other department heads expressed varying degrees of dissatisfaction with this new budgeting system.

Of the 13 department heads who were interviewed, only 2 (15 percent) expressed the opinion that there may have been some reallocation of financial resources as a result of information supplied to Mr. Carter by the new budgeting system during the reorganization of the Executive Branch of the state. However, they were unable to give a single instance in which the new budgeting system had reallocated resources in their own departments. The other 11 department heads (85 percent) indicated there had been no apparent reallocation of financial resources in their departments as a result of implementing zero-base budgeting.

Mr. Carter expressed a different opinion regarding the contribution of zero-base budgeting in reallocating financial resources in the state. In doing so, he said that he understood the negative responses of the department heads and departmental budget analysts on this issue since the contribution of the new budgeting system in this particular area would not be apparent to them. This was because the reallocation of financial resources was a result of a combination of two factors: (1.) the reorganization of the Executive Branch of state government and (2.) the manner in which the zero-base budgeting system was initially adopted and implemented.[12]

It is public knowledge in Georgia that there was a substantial reallocation of financial resources within state government during Mr. Carter's administration—especially during his first year in office. However, it was the Executive Reorganization Act of 1972 that has been credited with reallocating the state's financial resources during this period. The purpose of this act was to consolidate under a single authority similar state functions and programs that were previously controlled by different departments and activities throughout state government.

Mr. Carter agreed that it was the Executive Reorganization Act of 1972 that was the primary force in reallocating financial resources within the state. However, he also stated:

"The detection of need for consolidating similar functions within state government is made from the zero-base budgeting technique. It would have been virtually impossible to have made the change we did under the old incremental budgeting system. We have had such a profound change in the structure of government that most people attribute this shifting of roles and also shifting of resources to the reorganization itself which has been so much more present in our mind than to zero-base budgeting." [13]

Much of the dissatisfaction expressed by department heads with zero-base budgeting appeared to result from the way in which it was originally presented and later implemented. Only after the decision had been made to implement the new budgeting system did Mr. Carter hold a series of meetings with his department heads to explain the system and the reasons for its adoption. The fact that the department heads had no input into the original decision to adopt the zero-base budgeting system seemed to have a detrimental effect on their attitudes toward the system.

Budget Analysts' Reactions

Responses of departmental budget analysts regarding their perceptions of a number of areas were obtained:

Perceived Time, Effort, and Involvement Required Under New System. As would be expected, the time and effort required to convert from the incremental system to the zero-base budgeting system was perceived as being considerable (see part A, Exhibit 1). After the initial implementation, the time and effort was still perceived as being greater than under the incremental budgeting system (see part B, Exhibit 1).

One of the goals of a zero-base budgeting system is to achieve greater involvement of line personnel in the budgeting process. Exhibit 1, part C, shows that about 52 percent of the budget analysts believed that department heads became more involved than under the former incremental system. Part D shows that about 68 percent believed that first-line supervisors became more involved. Only one respondent indicated that there was less involvement by these persons. The OPB budget analysts perceived greater involvement by both agency heads and first-line supervisors than did the departmental analysts.

Adequacy of Planning, Instructions, and Cost Data. The results shown in Exhibit 2 indicate that 53 percent of the total respondents believed that the advanced planning was inadequate. Of the departmental analysts, 65 percent believed that advanced planning was inadequate, contrasted to only 22 percent of the OPB analysts who felt this way. Typical comments from departmental analysts were: "The system was designed for industry and not state government." "Each agency should have had time to work with the system to test it before it was implemented."

Although 36 percent of the respondents believed the instructions received during the first year were inadequate, only 9 percent believed they

Exhibit 5-1 Perceptions of Budget Analysts Regarding Time, Effort, and Involvement Required Under Zero-Base Budgeting
(Segregated as to Departmental Budget Analysts and Analysts in the Office of Planning and Budget)

	Departmental Budget Analysts		OPB Budget Analysts		Total	
	No.	Percent	No.	Percent	No.	Percent
A. What effect did the zero-base budgeting system have on the time and effort spent in budgeting preparation during the first year of its implementation?						
a. Increased considerably.	18	78.3%	7	87.5%	25	80.6%
b. Increased slightly.	5	21.7	1	12.5	6	19.4
c. Remained about the same.						
d. Decreased slightly.						
e. Decreased considerably.						
B. Now that the zero-based budgeting system has been implemented, how great is the time and effort spent in budget preparation in comparison to the previous incremental budgeting system?						
a. Much greater	10	43.5%	3	37.5%	13	41.9%
b. Slightly more.	7	30.4	4	50.0	11	35.5
c. About the same.	5	21.7			5	16.1
d. Slightly less.	1	4.4	1	12.5	2	6.5
e. Much less.						
C. Did the agency head become more involved in budget formulation after the implementation of zero-base budgeting?						
a. Much more involved.	5	21.7%	4	50.0%	9	29.0%
b. Slightly more involved.	5	21.7	2	25.0	7	22.6
c. About the same.	13	56.6	1	12.5	14	45.2
d. Slightly less involved.						
e. Much less involved.			1	12.5	1	3.2
D. Did first-line supervisors become involved in budget formulation after the implementation of zero-base budgeting?						
a. Much more involved.	10	43.5%	6	75.0%	16	51.6%
b. Slightly more involved.	4	17.4	1	12.5	5	16.1
c. About the same as before.	9	39.1			9	29.0
d. Slightly less involved.						
e. Much less involved.			1	12.5	1	3.2

Exhibit 5-2 Perceptions of Budget Analysts Regarding Adequacy of Planning, Instructions, and Cost Data

	Departmental Budget Analysts		OPB Budget Analysts		Total	
	No.	Percent	No.	Percent	No.	Percent
A. Do you feel adequate advanced planning on the part of the Budget Bureau was conducted before implementation of the new zero-base budgeting system?						
a. Yes.	4	17.4%	4	44.5%	8	25.0%
b. No.	15	65.2	2	22.2	17	53.1
c. Uncertain.	4	17.4	3	33.3	7	21.9
B. Do you feel you received adequate instructions during the first year of zero-base budgeting to properly prepare your budget requests?						
a. Yes.	11	47.8%	5	62.5%	16	51.6%
b. No.	10	43.5%	1	12.5	11	35.5
c. Uncertain.	2	8.7	2	25.0	4	12.9
C. Do you feel you presently have adequate instructions as to how to properly prepare a zero-base budget?						
a. Yes.	19	82.6%	8	88.9%	27	84.4%
b. No.	3	13.0			3	9.4
c. Uncertain.	1	4.4	1	11.1	2	6.2
D. During the first year of operating with the zero-base budgeting system, did you have adequate cost data available to properly prepare decision packages?						
a. Yes.	7	30.4%	2	25.0%	9	29.0%
b. No.	15	65.2	6	75.0	21	67.7
c. Uncertain.	1	4.4			1	3.2
E. Do you feel you presently have adequate cost data necessary to properly prepare a decision package?						
a. Yes.	15	65.2%	5	55.6%	20	62.5%
b. No.	7	30.4	3	33.3	10	31.2
c. Uncertain.	1	4.4	1	11.1	2	6.3

were inadequate after that period. Again, there was more dissatisfaction on the part of departmental analysts than by OPB analysts.

After the implementation of zero-base budgeting, it became apparent that budgeting guidelines were necessary to permit the budgetary process to proceed smoothly. Thus implementation of the zero-base system resulted in the creation of a planning phase prior to the preparation of the budget. Under the former incremental system the planning phase and budgeting phase were conducted concurrently. This change is seen as one of the advantages of adopting the new system.

Regarding cost data, 68 percent believed that adequate cost data were unavailable during the first year; 31 percent believed such cost data were unavailable after that period. It seems that problems with instructions and cost data were severe initially, but in time these problems were being resolved.

Quality of Management Information. One of the proposed benefits accruing from the use of a zero-base budgeting system is an increase in the quality of management information. The quality of management information under the new budgeting system as perceived by budget analysts is presented in Exhibit 3. Over half of the analysts (68 percent) indicated an improvement in the quality of management information. The degree of improvement was perceived as being much greater by the OPB budget analysts than by the departmental budget analysts.

Reallocation of Financial Resources. Another proposed benefit accruing from the installation of a zero-base budgeting system is that it would achieve a more efficient allocation of the state's financial resources. The effectiveness of zero-base budgeting in reallocating financial resources as perceived by budget analysts is shown in Exhibit 4. Only 7 percent perceived some shifting of financial resources as a result of the use of the new system.

In theory, zero-base budgeting should result in the immediate adjustment of the budget to changes in the level of funding. This is accomplished by preparing a decision-package ranking which lists all decision packages in order of their priority. After a level of funding is established, a cutoff line is employed to divide the decision packages between those to be approved and those to be disapproved. Any subsequent change in the level of funding should require only a shift in the position of the cutoff line.

However, the actual results obtained from this system have been disappointing. During fiscal year 1974, there was an increase in the availability of funds in the state. Instead of shifting the cutoff line downward to include more marginal decision packages, Governor Carter requested new

---

Exhibit 5-3 Quality of Management Information as Perceived by Budget Analysts

	Departmental Budget Analysts		OPB Budget Analysts		Total	
	No.	Percent	No.	Percent	No.	Percent
All good budgeting systems generate information for management planning and control. What effect did the zero-base budgeting system have on the quality of management information as compared to the previous incremental budgeting system?						
a. Quality of management information substantially improved.	3	13.1%	4	50.0%	7	22.6%
b. Quality of management information slightly improved.	11	47.8	3	37.5	14	45.2
c. About the same as before.	9	39.1	1	12.5	10	32.2
d. Quality of management information slightly decreased.						
e. Quality of management information substantially decreased.						

---

decision packages from some of his departments to help him allocate additional funds.

In fiscal year 1975 there was a reduction in the availability of funds originally projected for that year. Again, the decision-package ranking proved ineffective. Instead of raising the cutoff line to eliminate the lower priority decision packages, almost all departments had to resubmit a new decision-package ranking based on the lower level of funding. One departmental budget analyst summed up the problem by stating: "The priority ranking of our decision packages when we expect 140 percent funding simply is not the same as when we expect 115 percent funding."

Practicality of Preparing Decision Packages and Notification of Changes in Decision-Package Rankings. As used in this study, the term "decision package" is restricted to its application in a zero-base budgeting system.

Exhibit 5-4 The Effects of Zero-Base Budgeting on the Reallocation of the State's Financial Resources as Perceived by Budget Analysts

	Departmental Budget Analysts		OPB Budget Analysts		Total	
	No.	Percent	No.	Percent	No.	Percent
Did the implementation of the zero-base budgeting system cause a shifting of financial resources among functions in your agency?						
a. Large shifting of financial resources.						
b. Some shifting of financial resources.	4	17.4%	3	33.3%	7	21.9%
c. No apparent shifting of financial resources.	19	82.6	2	22.2	21	65.6
d. Uncertain.			4	44.5	4	12.5

The Zero-Base Budgeting Manual of the state of Georgia defines a decision package as "an identification of a discrete function or operation in a definitive manner for management evaluation and comparison to other functions, including consequences of not performing that function, alternative courses of action, and cost and benefits."[14]

Decision packages differ from programs because of the time frames involved. A program includes the projected financial data applicable throughout the program's life; the financial data included in a decision package refer only to the fiscal year under consideration.

Decision packages are used in zero-base budgeting systems in both industry and government, although the format of the packages differs slightly between the two types of organizations. Exhibit 5 is a sample of a decision package for use in the 1973 Fiscal Year Budget.

The preparation of decision packages is essential to the zero-base system. Each department or agency identifies various decision packages and the benefits expected, gives the costs of resources required, and lists the consequences of not funding the package (among other data). The packages then are ranked in order of decreasing benefit to the department or agency.

Responses of budget analysts regarding the practicality of preparing decision packages are given in Exhibit 6, part A. A total of 62.5 percent of all respondents and 74 percent of departmental budget analysts believed that it was not practical to prepare a decision package representing a minimum level of effort.

Exhibit 5-5 Sample Decision Package, 1973 Fiscal Year Budget

(1) Package Name Air Quality Laboratory (1 of 3)	(2) Agency Health	(3) Activity Air Quality Control	(4) Organization Ambient Air	(5) Rank 3

(6) Statement of Purpose

Ambient air laboratory analysis must be conducted for identification and evaluation of pollutants by type and by volume. Sample analysis enables engineers to determine effect of control and permits use of an emergency warning system.

(7) Description of Actions (Operations)

Use a central lab to conduct all sample testing and analysis: 1 Chemist II, 1 Chemist I, 2 Technicians, and 1 Steno I. This staff could analyze and report on a maximum of 37,300 samples. At 37,300 samples per year, we would only sample the 5 major urban areas of the state (70% of the population). These 5 people are required as a minimum to conduct comprehensive sample analysis of even a few samples on a continuous basis.

(8) Achievement from Actions

Ambient air laboratory analysis yields valuable information for management and field engineers to enable them to evaluate effects on the Air Quality Program, identify new or existing pollutants by type and volume, and maintain an emergency warning system.

(9) Consequences of Not Approving Package

Field engineers would be forced to rely on their portable testing equipment which does not provide the desired quantitative data (the portable equipment only identifies pollutants by major type, does not measure particle size, and does not provide quantitative chemical analyses to determine the specific chemical compounds in the pollutant), and greatly reduces the effectiveness of the emergency warning system which requires detailed quantitative chemical analyses.

Exhibit 5-5 Continued

(10) Quantitative Package Measures	FY 1971	FY 1972	FY 1973
Samples analyzed & reported	38,000	55,000	37,300
Cost per sample	$4.21	$4.07	$3.75
Samples per man hour	3.8	3.9	3.7

(11) Resources Required ($ in Thousands)	FY 1971	FY 1972	FY 1973	% FY 73/72
Operational	160	224	140	63%
Grants				
Capital Outlay				
Lease Rentals				
Total	160	224	140	63%
People (Positions)	5	7	5	71%

Manager_____   Prepared By_____   Date_____   Page 1 of___2___

Exhibit 5-5 Continued

(1) Package Name Air Quality Laboratory (1 of 3)	(2) Agency Health	(3) Activity Air Quality Control	(4) Organization Ambient Air	(5) Rank 3

(12) Alternatives (Different Levels of Effort) and Cost

Air Quality Laboratory (2 of 3): $61K*—Analyze 27,700 additional samples (totaling 55,000 samples, which is the current level), thereby determining air quality for 5 additional problem urban areas and 8 other counties chosen on the basis of worst pollution (covering 80% of the population).

Air Quality Laboratory (3 of 3): $45K—Analyze 20,000 additional samples (totaling 75,000 samples), thereby determining air quality for 90% of the population, and leaving only rural areas with little or no pollution problems unsampled.

*(Note: $61K = $61,000)

(13) Alternatives (Different Ways of Performing the Same Function, Activity, or Operation)

1. Contract sample analysis work to Georgia Tech—Cost $6 per sample for a total cost of $224K for analyzing 37,300 samples. Emergency warning system would not be as effective due to their time requirement on reporting analysis work done by graduate students.

2. Conduct sample analysis work entirely in regional locations—cost a total of $506K the first year and $385K in subsequent years. Specialized equipment must be purchased in the first year for several locations if central lab is discontinued. Subsequent years would also require lab staffing at several locations at minimum levels which would not fully utilize people.

3. Conduct sample analysis work in central lab for special pollutants only, and set up regional labs to reduce sample mailing costs—cost a total of $305K for analyzing 37,300 samples. Excessive cost would persist due to minimum lab staffing at several locations in addition to the special central lab.

Exhibit 5-5 Continued

(14) Source of Funds ($ in Thousands)	FY 1971	FY 1972	FY 1973
Federal			
Operational: Other			
State			
Grants: Federal			
State			
Capital and Lease: Federal			
State			

(15) Projection of Funds Committed by This Package	Funds	FY 1974	FY 1975	FY 1976	FY 1977	FY 1978
	State					
	Total					

Reasons:

As for notification of changes in the rankings of decision packages at the executive level, 74 percent (see Exhibit 6, part B) said they were notified always or most of the time. It would seem desirable that notification always be given when changes in the rankings are made.

Future Use of Zero-Base Budgeting System. Exhibit 7 presents a summary of the responses of budget analysts regarding the advisability of continuing the zero-base budgeting system in the state.

Of the respondents, 84 percent recommended the continued use of zero-base budgeting in some form. This is somewhat surprising because most of the preliminary interviews with budget analysts seemed to reveal a great deal of dissatisfaction with the new budgeting system. This dissatisfaction also was reflected, to a lesser degree, by the responses to various questions in the questionnaire.

While expressing dissatisfaction with many parts of the zero-base budgeting system, most analysts concede that there has been a basic improvement in the budgeting process as a result of implementing the new budget-

Exhibit 5-6 Perceptions of Budget Analysts Regarding the Preparation and Notification of Changes in Ranking of Decision Packages

	Departmental Budget Analysts		OPB Budget Analysts		Total	
	No.	Percent	No.	Percent	No.	Percent
A. Presently you are required to prepare decision packages representing different levels of effort for each function. Do you feel it is practical to prepare a decision package representing a minimum level of effort?						
a. Yes.	6	26.1%	5	55.6%	11	34.3%
b. No.	17	73.9	3	33.3	20	62.5
c. No opinion.			1	11.1	1	3.1
B. After your agency has submitted its decision-package rankings for executive review, are you notified of any changes in these rankings and the reasons for the change?						
a. Always.	8	34.8%	2	25.0%	10	32.3%
b. Most of the time.	9	39.1	4	50.0	13	41.9
c. Seldom.	2	8.7	2	25.0	4	12.9
d. Never.	4	17.4			4	12.9

Exhibit 5-7 Opinions of Departmental Budget Analysts Regarding the Future Use of Zero-Base Budgeting

	Departmental Budget Analysts		OPB Budget Analysts		Total	
	No.	Percent	No.	Percent	No.	Percent
This study is very interested in your opinion of the zero-base budgeting system. Which of the following alternatives do you feel is in the best interest of the state of Georgia?						
a. Continue the zero-base budgeting system substantially as it operates today.	5	21.7%	5	55.6%	10	31.3%
b. Continue the zero-base budgeting system with some major modifications.	10	43.5	2	22.2	12	37.5
c. Continue the zero-base budgeting system except that it not be employed every year.	3	13.1	2	22.2	5	15.6
d. Discontinue the zero-base budgeting system.	5	21.7			5	15.6

ing system. Also, the opinion was expressed that it was better to continue the present system rather than have to learn a new system or relearn the incremental budgeting system.

Conclusions

Three primary advantages appear to be associated with the employment of the zero-base budgeting system in the state of Georgia.

The first advantage concerns the establishment of a financial planning phase prior to the preparation of the fiscal year budget. Before the implementation of zero-base budgeting, the planning phase was conducted concurrently with the budgeting phase. As a result, there were no budgetary guidelines available during the budget preparation. After the implementation of zero-base budgeting it became apparent that some budgetary guidelines were necessary to properly allocate the state's limited financial resources in such a way as to best satisfy the goals and objectives of the state.

The second advantage concerns an improvement in the quality of management information resulting from the employment of the zero-base budgeting system. The use of this new budgeting system has enabled the governor, department heads, departmental budget analysts, and budget analysts in the Office of Planning and Budget to have a much greater insight into the functions of state government.

The third advantage of employing the zero-base budgeting system has been an increase in the involvement of personnel at the activity level in the state's budgeting process. Before zero-base budgeting, most of the input into the budgeting process came from the departmental budget analysts. After the new budgeting system was implemented, activity managers were required to prepare and rank decision packages, thus providing input into the budgeting process.

The major disadvantage associated with the employment of the zero-base budgeting system in the state appears to be the increased time and effort required for budget preparation. This is a very serious problem, and it has contributed to some of the dissatisfaction with the new system, particularly among personnel at the department and activity level. This dissatisfaction, in turn, has had a detrimental effect on the effectiveness of the zero-base budgeting system. Quite possibly the amount of time and effort required will decrease significantly as all persons become more familiar with the new system.

The study indicates that there have been two other significant shortcomings associated with the employment of zero-base budgeting in the state of Georgia. These are: (1) the contention that the new budgeting system to date has not significantly affected the efficient allocation of the state's financial resources and (2) the seeming ineffectiveness of the decision-package ranking in meeting changes in the level of fundings. However, the previous system also included these same shortcomings. Possibly, as those involved gain more experience in preparing and ranking decision packages, these shortcomings will be eliminated. On balance, the implementation of zero-base budgeting appears to have served the best interests of the state of Georgia.

NOTES

1. Peter A. Phyrr, "Zero-Base Budgeting," *Harvard Business Review,* November-December 1970, pp. 111–121.
2. Jimmy Carter, *State of the State Address,* unpublished speech presented to the Joint Session of the General Assembly of Georgia, Atlanta, Georgia, January 11, 1972.
3. Ibid.
4. Jimmy Carter, *Budget Address to the Joint Session of the General Assembly of Georgia,* unpublished speech presented to the Joint Session of the General Assembly of Georgia, Atlanta, Georgia, January 13, 1972.
5. Ibid.

6. S. Kenneth Howard, "Changing Concepts of State Budgeting," *Approaches to the State Central Budget Process* (Lexington, Kentucky, National Association of State Budget Officers, 1970), p. 5.

7. Charles E. Lindblom, "Decision-Making in Taxation and Expenditure," *Public Finances: Needs, Sources, and Utilization* (Princeton, New Jersey, Princeton University Press, 1961), pp. 297-298.

8. Peter Phyrr, "Zero-Base Budgeting," unpublished speech delivered to the international conference of the Planning Executives Institute, New York Hilton Hotel, May 15, 1972.

9. U.S. Congress, Senate Committee on Government Operations, Subcommittee on National Policy Machinery, *Hearings Organizing for National Security: The Budget and the Policy Process,* 87th Congress, 1st Session, 1961, p. 1107.

10. Governor Jimmy Carter, interview held in the Governor's Office, State Capitol Building, Atlanta, Georgia, January 7, 1974.

11. Ibid.

12. Ibid.

13. Ibid.

14. *Zero-Base Budgeting Manual—Fiscal Year 1973 Budget Development,* State of Georgia (March 15, 1971), p. 2.

Chapter 6

Final Considerations

In the planning stages of this work, I realized that the final product would not be the first nor, perhaps, the last one written on the subject of zero-base budgeting. My task was to provide the health care manager with a compendium of information that detailed the zero-base technique and gave an insight into the attempts of others through case studies. Furthermore, since business literature has included professional papers on the subject, an exposure to what business executives, managers, and academics are discovering about zero-base would be helpful. Another purpose is to present clearly the features of zero-base budgeting so the financial manager can make an intelligent decision about whether to adopt the process. For institutions whose administration deems zero-base to be advantageous, I offer some final considerations that may be beneficial.

Many executives who install a new management technique in their organizations will look back after several years and say, "It would have been much easier if I had contracted with a consulting firm." Caution: many individuals and firms are offering their services as consultants on zero-base systems and their quality ranges from superior to suspect. When contracting with consultants, management should obtain a list of clients who have used their services for installing zero-base procedures and ask their opinions. If someone at an organization that has used the consultant is known, their opinion should be sought. If the consultant is hesitant about giving names of clients, management should request client case studies with name changes to protect their confidentiality. With the number of private companies and governmental units using zero-base budgeting growing steadily, finding well-qualified consultants should be no great problem.

Along with the increase in zero-base consultants is the growth in the number of packaged zero-base programs. These canned programs are general enough so that some of their features will be adaptable to any health care institution, but the entire program cannot be used by any organization with complete success. Packaged systems often are computerized, so their applicability to a specific institution is analogous to applying statistical data regarding the "average American family with 1.6 children" to one's own family. It just doesn't fit exactly. There are no quick ways to a successful zero-base budgeting system. It takes considerable time and effort on the part of the management staff.

Another consideration concerns a caveat mentioned in earlier chapters, but its importance cannot be overemphasized and bears repeating. Before implementation of zero-base—or even the thought of adoption—the chief administrative officer must be in total agreement with and support of the concept. The administrator should be involved from the issuance of the initial directive through, for example, the ranking process as a moderator of the ranking committee. The administrator's zero-base duties should include directing a review of the process after each budget has been completed. The review will help management focus on deficiencies in the system that may be ironed out before the next year's cycle begins.

A last consideration is one that has plagued zero-base budgeting since its popularity grew with Carter's election as President. Many persons inside or outside of health care organizations believe zero-base budgeting is simply a fad and will not be used for long as a management tool in the private and public sectors. Like PPBS, initiated by Robert S. McNamara in the Department of Defense, zero-base budgeting will be fashionable for a time but will meet its demise shortly, these persons contend. The line of reasoning that zero-base is a fad or fashion is not sustained by empirical evidence. Numerous corporations have used zero-base and have reported successful results that encourage its continued use. State and local governments are using zero-base budgeting and many are applauding its advantages as a decision-making tool. Furthermore, considerable critical thinking and writing on zero-base has helped streamline the process and make it more sophisticated.

The thought process promoted by zero-base budgeting is not new or unique. Business decisions considering the cost to the organization and the benefits to be derived from that cost are made routinely. Therefore, even if zero-base budgeting does not survive in its present form, its formalized approach to the difficult art of decision making will make valuable contributions to health care organizational management.

Appendix A

INITIAL STEPS TOWARD IMPLEMENTING A ZERO-BASE SYSTEM

Persons who will be responsible for preparing decision packages for their units should be completely familiar with the package format and the information they will be required to supply. The department heads and decision unit managers should be educated in some formal sense both as a group and individually so there will be little misunderstanding or lack of uniformity. One way of presenting formal instruction is a series of meetings at which the budget supervisor will lead the department head through the decision package forms. The meeting agendas may follow the suggestions below. The objective of the meetings is not only to familiarize the department heads with the zero-base process and its purposes but also to ease their burden when developing decision packages and, further, to produce some uniformity between packages submitted by various departments.

CONFERENCE 1

Suggested Agenda*

Purpose: Discuss the basic zero-base system as it relates to resource allocation.

This meeting is to get the manager in the proper frame of mind so that the person's first attempt at the "homework" will be a written articulation of the discussion.

---

*Plan for 1 to 2 hours per meeting with each department head.

1. Discuss with department head any questions about the conceptual nature of the system.
2. Discuss the following points about the department:
   a. The organization (this will help identify decision units)
   b. The purpose of the department
   c. The history of the department and its management
   d. With what other departments or people must the unit coordinate and interact?
   e. Does the department use performance measures to determine effectiveness and efficiency?
   f. What personnel and physical resources are being used?
   g. What demands for services are being experienced and what growth pattern is anticipated?

Ask the department head to take some blank forms (A and B attached) and "rough" out some answers to each section numbered 7, 8, 9, 10, and 11 for the next meeting.

DECISION UNIT SUMMARY

FORM A

| (1) DECISION UNIT NAME: | (2) DEPARTMENT: | (3) PREPARER: | (4) DATE: | (5) REVIEWER: | DATE: |

(6) SUMMARY OF INCREMENTAL REQUESTS FOR 19B.

(a) SERVICE PROVIDED.

Increment Number	% of 19A Level	INCREMENTAL			CUMULATIVE		
		EXPENSE	FTEs		EXPENSE	%	FTEs	%
1 of							
2 of							
3 of							
of							
of							
of							

(b) 19A ACTUAL EXPENSES AND EMPLOYEES.

(7) OBJECTIVE OF THE DECISION UNIT:

(8) CURRENT OPERATIONS AND RESOURCES USED:

(9) ALTERNATIVE MEANS TO ACCOMPLISH OBJECTIVE (SHOW WHY REJECTED OR ACCEPTED. INDICATE ANY REMAINING ON PENDING LIST.)

(10) CRITICAL RELATIONSHIPS WITH OTHER DEPARTMENTS OR DECISION UNITS.

DECISION UNIT INCREMENT

FORM B

INCREMENT ___ of ___

| (1) DECISION UNIT NAME: | (2) DEPARTMENT: | (3) PREPARER: | (4) DATE: | (5) REVIEWER: | DATE: |

(11) RESOURCES NEEDED

19 B BUDGET

	INCREMENT		CUMULATIVE		
	EXPENSE	EMPLOYEE	EXPENSE	% 19A	EMPLOYEE	%19A
(a) INCREMENT RESOURCES NEEDED						
(b) DECISION UNIT RESOURCES USED IN 19A						

(12) INCREMENTAL SERVICES PROVIDED:

(13) CONSEQUENCES OF NOT FUNDING OR, IF NO. 1 INCREMENT, WHY NOT A LOWER LEVEL.

(14) PLANNED WORKLOAD AND PERFORMANCE

	19 A ACTUAL	19 B	
		INCREMENT	CUMULATIVE
SERVICE DEMAND			
QUALITY			
QUANTITY			

CONFERENCE 2

Purpose: Establish a definite purpose and the expected services to be offered by the department.

Cover in detail each question and the department head's responses. The following are suggested areas to probe.

Question 7: Objectives

a. The statement should not be a list of current activities but a statement of purpose.
b. The objectives should be subject to some performance measures.
c. The statement should indicate what the department will do with the resources given to it.

Question 8: Current Operations

a. Are the resources required to support the current activities justified? The resources should be adequate with no "fat".
b. What resources used are outside the department head's control? What coordination is necessary between organizational units?

Question 9: Alternatives

a. Explore alternatives that may have been overlooked or avoided if the department head has listed none.
b. Discuss reasonable alternatives to some that were rejected. Be sure narrative on decision package is sufficient to support rejection.
c. Discuss any possibilities that may be considered for the future even though not viable now.

Question 10: Critical Relationships

a. Discuss and document the effects on services or outputs if an expansion or a contraction of departmental funding occurred.
b. Discuss and document any effects on services and outputs if an expansion or a contraction of other departments' funding occurs.

Question 11: Measures of Performance

a. Select objectives susceptible to some performance measures that may be objective (such as cost standards) or subjective (such as ranking from superior to poor).

b. Isolate a specific performance measure with a particular objective.

The department head should be able to improve the decision packages for more meaningful comparisons and trade-off decisions.

For the next conference, have the department manager rewrite all questions above and rough out Questions 12 and 13 on Form B.

CONFERENCE 3

Purpose: Begin draft forms.

Question 12: Incremental Service from Package Request

a. Narrate only the service provided from the package request; there should be no accumulation of services from previous package requests.
b. Articulate clearly the statement of services to be provided from this package alone to facilitate ranking.

Question 13: Consequences of Not Funding

a. Indicate, for the minimum increment (just keeping the doors open), a minimum resource request for a minimum amount of service.
b. Show that the consequences of not funding the request always should lead to a less attractive alternative.

The department head should be ready to begin drafting decision packages.

A key point to cover in the third conference is the department head's concept of incrementalization.

a. Inquire about the minimum level of funding and whether it really will work with the amount requested.
b. Point out that each package must indicate the costs and benefits for that amount of resources only.
c. Remind the department head that each package must stand on its own merits when being ranked against others presented by other managers.

Ask for a final draft of all forms, including the ranking.

FORM C

19 B PROPOSED BUDGET

| (1) DECISION UNIT NAME: | (2) DEPARTMENT: | (3) PREPARER: | (4) DATE: | (5) REVIEWER: | DATE: |

ACCOUNT NUMBER	DESCRIPTION	19 A ACTUAL	19 B PROPOSED INCREMENTS				19 B TOTAL INCREMENTS	19 B APPROVED BUDGET
			1 of	2 of	3 of	4 of		
	FTEs MANAGEMENT STAFF							

Appendix B

by Dean Grant and Bruce Fisher

THE ALEXIAN BROTHERS MEDICAL CENTER

A Descriptive Case of Zero-Base Budgeting in Action

The following material is a comprehensive review of the design, implementation, and effects of a zero-base budgeting system at The Alexian Brothers Medical Center in Chicago. The administration's initial memoranda to department heads give valuable insights into the type of information that may be transmitted before the process is initiated. Following the memoranda and forms sent to the staff is the narrative reporting management's thought processes before beginning the system, then the implementation and results of the zero-base system. Several cases and exhibits are presented to explain individual difficulties associated with the process and specific examples of how department heads used zero-base budgeting.

This case should not be viewed as an ideal methodology of installing and using a zero-base system. Instead, it should be read as a learning tool that will assist other health care institutions in establishing their own systems. It is the author's view, however, that this was a well-thought-out, well-conceived zero-base system from the beginning; but as can be seen, it is impossible to design a system without some pitfalls or problems.

MEMORANDA FROM THE ADMINISTRATION TO DEPART-MENT HEADS LEADING UP TO INSTALLATION OF THE ZERO-BASE BUDGETING PROCESS AT THE ALEXIAN BROTHERS MEDICAL CENTER

ALEXIAN BROTHERS MEDICAL CENTER   Interoffice Memorandum

TO: Department Heads

FROM: Administration

DATE:

SUBJECT: Zero-Based Budgeting Package

Attached is the ZBB package for the 19___ Fiscal Year. This package represents our adherence to a request from our Board of Trustees that the Medical Center try the ZBB approach.

There are four sections to this package and each one should be reviewed in order to understand the ZBB concept. Only after you have reviewed each section should you begin. Then, you have to start with Section I and work forward.

Section I . . . . Overview, Objectives and Organizational Chart
Section II . . . . Developing Decision Units
Section III . . . . Evaluate and Rank All Decision Packages
Section IV . . . . Ten Examples of Decision Units and Their Prioritizing

Since the ZBB approach is new to the Medical Center, there are bound to be many questions. Please see your supervisor for assistance.

BF/gl

ALEXIAN BROTHERS MEDICAL CENTER   Interoffice Memorandum

TO: Department Heads

FROM: Administration

DATE:

SUBJECT: Zero-Based Budgeting Package
           Section I: Overview, Objectives and Organizational Chart

Background Leading to Zero-Base Planning and Budgeting. Although the buzz words "zero-base budgeting" are relatively new to many managers, the underlying concept is nothing more than a "systemization" of the operational planning and budgeting decision processes you have used for years. In fact, the "zero-base" technique is primarily a planning tool and a budgeting tool secondarily. Planning and budgeting must work hand in hand as part of the managerial process of accomplishing work assignments and objectives in a cost-effective manner. Plans developed without adequate consideration of the dollars and personnel required to carry them out are as useless as budgets prepared without consideration of the organizational, procedural and other operational factors that need to be *controlled* to make the budgets realistic targets.

Zero-Based Budgeting Approach

(1) Set goals and objectives.
(2) Evaluate current activities and alternatives.
(3) Identify new activities and alternatives.
(4) Establish priorities before detail number work is done.
(5) Test against plans.
(6) Establish trade-offs, reallocate resources according to priorities.
(7) Budget and operating plan established.
(8) Compile detailed budgets.

Benefits of ZBB. ZBB provides top management with detailed information concerning the money needed to accomplish desired ends, *and*:

(1) Spotlights duplication of efforts among departments.
(2) Focuses on dollars needed for programs rather than on percentage change from previous year.

(3) Specifies priorities within and among departments and divisions.
(4) Allows comparisons of priorities across organizational lines.
(5) Allows a performance audit to determine whether each activity and operation is performed as promised.

Prior to starting your Zero-Based Budget, you should list the objectives you wish to accomplish in 19__. These objectives should be listed in numerical order in the priority you establish. Use Schedule A for listing these objectives.

In order to accomplish your objectives, an organizational chart is necessary. The organizational chart should depict your department in a functional approach. Names are not to be used, but the number of full-time equivalents by function is required. In many instances, an organizational chart is already available and only needs minor updating.

BF/gl

S A M P L E
ALEXIAN BROTHERS MEDICAL CENTER

Department Name: Controller's Office   19___ Departmental Objectives   Department No.:   901

(1) Provide the Board of Trustees, Finance Committee, and Administrative staff with current, accurate, and informative data in which to make financial decisions.

(2) Minimize the cost of performing the General Accounting functions while maximizing the department's efficiency.

(3) Provide middle management with current, accurate, and informative data in which to make daily operating decisions.

(4) Safeguard the assets of the institution.

(5) Update job descriptions for all functions in the Data Processing Department.

(6) Update the written documentation for all Payroll procedures.

(7) Develop a project cost report that summarizes the status of the current projects under construction.

(8) Explore the possibility of installing an interfaced computer system in Pharmacy. This will reduce the present double-handling of unit dose Pharmacy charges.

(9) Format a monthly direct cost departmental income statement.

(10) Confirm the existence and location of the movable equipment recorded on the appraisal reports by testing a random sample.

(11)

(12)

(13)

(14)

(15)

(16)

ALEXIAN BROTHERS MEDICAL CENTER

Department Name: _____   Department No.: _____

19___ Departmental Objectives

(1) _____

(2) _____

(3) _____

(4) _____

(5) _____

(6) _____

(7) _____

(8) _____

(9) _____

(10) _____

(11) _____

(12) _____

(13) _____

(14) _____

(15) _____

(16) _____

ALEXIAN BROTHERS MEDICAL CENTER ORGANIZATIONAL CHART

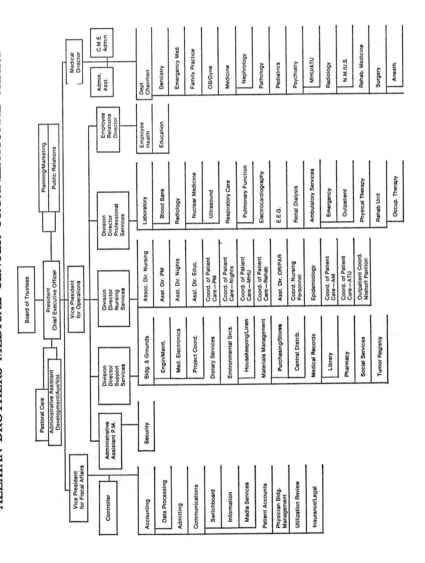

ALEXIAN BROTHERS MEDICAL CENTER   Interoffice Memorandum

TO: Department Heads

FROM: Administration

DATE:

SUBJECT: Zero-Based Budgeting Package
.   Section II: Developing Decision Units

The basic steps to be performed are:

(1) Identify "decision units".
(2) Analyze each "decision unit" in a series of "decision packages".

Step No. 1—Identify Decision Units. A "decision unit" is a tangible activity or group of activities, for which a single manager. has performance responsibility. There is no set method of identifying a "decision unit". The exhibit below shows a variety of ways of categorizing efforts into decision units; the obvious common feature of a unit is that there be some obvious, measurable output resulting from personnel and dollars committed to the unit in a budget year. Therefore, a *constraint* on how a decision unit is defined is that there exists, either in the accounting system or in an informal reporting system, a means of periodically measuring physical progress and resources consumed.

Traditional Cost Center

- Budget unit
- Most commonly used
- May be subdivided

People

- Accounting staff
- Accounts payable

Projects

- Computer system
- CAT scanner

Service Provided or Received

- Quality assurance
- Computer service
- Legal counsel

Objective of Expenditure

- Lease payments
- Professional fees

Capital

- Labor saving equipment project
- Office space project
- Etc.

Cost Reduction or Revenue Enhancement in Future Year

- Reorganization
- New procedures
- Training and development
- Etc.

Step No. 2—Analyze Each "Decision Unit" in a Series of "Decision Packages." This step is the heart of the operational planning activity. It results in a series of succinct, documented decisions concerning the activities to be performed in the budget year. Each decision package provides sufficient information concerning a planned activity to permit a manager and his supervisor to reach agreement as to whether the activity should be continued or eliminated, continued at the same level of effort or modified, continued to be performed in the same manner, or be replaced by a more cost-effective alternative. There are two classes of alternatives to be evaluated:
  (1) Different ways of performing the same function.
  (2) Different levels of effort in performing the same function.
     • Minimum (below current)
     • Additional levels or increments as decision packages

Why Different Levels of Effort?

  (1) Only limited funds are available.
     a. If only one level is identified, some activities or programs would be eliminated or arbitrarily reduced.
     b. Management may prefer to have option of reducing levels rather than entire programs or activities.
     c. Management can readily shift resources, increasing programs of high priority, while decreasing or eliminating programs of low priority.
  (2) Department managers are best equipped to identify and evaluate different levels.
     a. Provides better analysis of each operation.
     b. It then becomes top management's responsibility to rank.

Minimum Level of Effort

  (1) Must be below the current level of effort.
  (2) Should identify critical level of effort, below which the program or activity should be discontinued because it loses viability.
     a. May not completely achieve the objective.
     b. Should address itself to the most critical group being served or the most serious problem.
     c. May merely reduce the level of service.
     d. May imply operating improvements, organization changes and improvements in efficiency.
     e. May be any combination of the above.

The Decision Package Form with instructions on how to complete is attached. Before starting to develop Decision Packages, please review the examples in Section IV.

BF/gl

ALEXIAN BROTHERS MEDICAL CENTER

Filling Out Decision Package:

(1) Enter date submitted by initiating supervisor or manager.

(2) If Decision Package consists of (or relates to) an objective included in an organization plan, enter objective identification number.

(3) Enter short title of the activity or organization objective.

(4) Indicate level of effort here. For example, if the Decision Package represents the "minimum" increment of a three-level activity, enter "level 1 of 3".

(5-6) Self-explanatory.

(7) Enter the signature (or initials) of the initiating supervisor/ manager and of others in the approval chain. Generally, each Decision Package should be approved (with respect to correctness of information) by a department level executive.

(8) Enter Priority Ranking assigned to the Decision Package. Entry should be made in pencil to permit reranking at higher consolidation levels. Assign rank No. 1 to highest priority package.

(9) Describe the activity in terms of its purpose or intended result.

(10) Describe the activity in terms of the means or process by which the activity is to be accomplished.

(11) Where different ways of performing the activity have been evaluated, briefly describe the alternatives and the reasons why they were rejected. For example, if the Decision Package provides for the performance of a service in-house, why was the outside purchase rejected?

(12) State the principal benefits that will accrue to the hospital if the activity is retained (funded). Describe benefits to your own organization *and* other organizations that are affected.

(13) State the consequences that will result if the activity is eliminated (not funded). Distinguish between the consequences in your own organization and those in another organization.

(14-18) Fill in all applicable figures for budget year. If current year (expected) information is not readily available, provide reasonable estimate. To avoid misinterpretation, identify all data representing a partial year by indicating the number of months in parentheses. Round dollar figures to the nearest $100.

(14) Enter the number of employees (or equivalent employees) required to perform the activity.

(15) Enter the payroll costs of the activity.

(16) Enter the cost of major outside services, if any. Minor outside services should be included in No. 17.

(17) Enter the amount of other costs here.

(18) Total should equal the sum of No. 15, No. 16, and No. 17.

DECISION PACKAGE

OBJECTIVE NO. _____ (2)   DATE _____ (1)

ACTIVITY (OR OBJECTIVE) NAME (3)	LEVEL NO. (4) OF	DEPARTMENT (5)	PREPARED (7)	RANK (8)
		DIVISION (6)	APPROVED	

RESOURCES REQUIRED	CURRENT YEAR	BUDGET YEAR
PERSONNEL		
LABOR ($)		(14)
OUTSIDE SERVICES ($)		(15)
OTHER ($)		(16)
TOTAL ($)		(17)
		(18)

PURPOSE OF ACTIVITY

(9)

DESCRIPTION OF ACTIVITY

(10)

ALTERNATIVE WAYS OF PERFORMING WORK OR PROGRAM AND COSTS:

(11)

ADVANTAGES OF RETAINING ACTIVITY

(12)

CONSEQUENCES IF ACTIVITY IS ELIMINATED

(13)

DECISION PACKAGE   Date _____

ACTIVITY (OR OBJECTIVE) NAME	DEPARTMENT		PREPARED		RANK
LEVEL NO. ____ OF ____	DIVISION		APPROVED		

STATEMENT OF WORK OR PROGRAM	RESOURCES REQUIRED	CURRENT YEAR	BUDGET YEAR
	Personnel		
	Labor $		
	Outside Services $		
	Other $		
	Total $		

ALTERNATIVE WAYS OF PERFORMING WORK OR PROGRAM AND COSTS

ADVANTAGES OF RETAINING ACTIVITY

CONSEQUENCES IF ACTIVITY IS ELIMINATED

ALEXIAN BROTHERS MEDICAL CENTER   Interoffice Memorandum

TO: Department Heads

FROM: Administration

DATE:

SUBJECT: Zero-Based Budgeting Package
            Section III: Evaluate and Rank All Decision Packages

The basic steps to be performed are:

(1) Evaluate and rank all Decision Packages.
(2) Prepare detailed budget based on ranked Decision Packages.

Step one involves an assessment of the relative priorities of all activities and objectives proposed to be performed during the budget year. The prioritization is performed initially by the manager responsible for the budget. Subsequently, it is reviewed with his supervisor and various adjustments are agreed to. As part of the review and evaluation process, low priority packages are screened by an officer for departments under his jurisdiction to determine possible trade-offs among departments and reprioritization of the more discretionary items. Finally, the Ranking Forms and low priority Decision Packages are presented to the Budget Committee for discussion, evaluation of relative merits on a hospital-wide basis, and finally, determination of lowest priorities and total budget level for each department.

At the department level where the plan and budget originate, the responsible manager should rank all the activities he is responsible for in 1-2-3 order, from highest to lowest priority. He can do this by simply sorting the Decision Packages like a deck of cards and then placing a priority number on each page in sequence. If he wishes, he can instead use a "weighting system" to quantify the relative merits of a Decision Package.

Two problem areas should be avoided during the review and ranking process:
(1) Managers should not concentrate their time on activities that are legally or operationally required (other than to insure that all alternatives, cost reduction opportunities, and operating improvements

have been explored and incorporated as appropriate), but should concentrate on discretionary activities.

(2) Managers should not spend too much time worrying whether activity 4 is more important than activity 5, but only assure themselves that activities 4 and 5 are more important than activity 15, and activity 15 more important than 25, etc.

Filling Out Ranking Form:

The Ranking Form with instructions on how to complete is attached.

A typical Ranking Form is displayed in Section IV and should be reviewed.

Step No. 2, preparing detailed budgets based on Ranked Decision Packages, is the last step and should be the same as the incremental budget package that is turned in to your supervisor.

BF/gl

ALEXIAN BROTHERS MEDICAL CENTER

Filling Out Priority Ranking Form:

(1) Enter date prepared by initiating supervisor or manager.

(2-3) Self-explanatory.

(4) Signature or initials of individual preparing the Ranking Form if other than the approving supervisor or manager.

(5) Signature or initials of supervisor or manager approving the rankings shown on the form.

(6) Self-explanatory.

(7) Must agree with ranking displayed on each Decision Package Form. First entry should be priority No. 1.

(8) Enter name of Activity from No. 3 of each Decision Package. If name is not sufficiently self-explanatory, underline name and add brief description summarized from No. 9 and No. 10 of the Decision Package.

(9) Package level number obtained from No. 4 of each Decision Package.

(10) Organization objective number, if applicable, obtained from No. 2 of each Decision Package.

(11-12) Personnel figures obtained from No. 14 of each Decision Package.

(13-14) Dollar figures obtained from No. 18 of each Decision Package.

(15) Enter cumulative total of budget year dollars.

(16-20) On each page of the Ranking Form, enter cumulative column totals as appropriate. Cumulative totals on last page will constitute grand totals.

PRIORITY RANKING FORM

DATE _____

①

DEPARTMENT ②	DIVISION ③					PREPARED ④ APPROVED ⑤			PAGE ⑥ OF

	ACTIVITY				CURRENT YEAR			BUDGET YEAR	
RANK	NAME AND DESCRIPTION	LEVEL NO. OF NO.	ORG. OBJ. NO.		PERS.	$ (000)	PERS.	$ (000)	CUMULA-TIVE $ (000)
⑦	⑧	⑨	⑩		⑪	⑫	⑬	⑭	⑮
	TOTALS				⑯	⑰	⑱	⑲	⑳

PRIORITY RANKING

Date   August 25, 19____

DEPARTMENT	DIVISION	PREPARED
Accounting	Finance	APPROVED

PAGE 1
OF 1

ACTIVITY			CURRENT YEAR		BUDGET YEAR		
RANK	NAME AND DESCRIPTION	LEVEL NO. OF NO.	PER-SONNEL	$ (000)	PER-SONNEL	$ (000)	CUMULA-TIVE $ (000)
1	Accounting Budget Analysis	1 — 3	2	26,880	2	29,166	29,166
2	Personnel Budget Analysis	1 — 3	1	16,895	1	18,093	47,259
3	Controller's Office	1 — 2	1	10,402	1	11,988	59,247
4	Accounting Budget Analysis	2 — 3	1	21,090	1	22,878	82,125
5	Personnel Budget Analysis	2 — 3	3	52,538	3.6	60,152	142,277
6	Controller's Office	2 — 2	1	27,480	1	29,688	171,965
7	Accounting Budget Analysis	3 — 3	0	0	1.3	21,850	193,815
8	Personnel Budget Analysis	3 — 3	0	0	0.8	15,504	209,319
9	Staff Support	1 — 2	1	15,930	1	22,888	232,207
10	Staff Support	2 — 2	0	0	0.3	4,705	236,912
TOTALS			10	171,215	13	236,912	

(See page 244 for blank form)

ALEXIAN BROTHERS MEDICAL CENTER   Interoffice Memorandum

TO: Department Heads

FROM: Administration

DATE:

SUBJECT: Zero-Based Budgeting Package
         Section IV: Examples of Decision Packages and Priority
         Ranking

Attached are examples of decision packages for various activities in the Controller's Office.

Activity	Decision Packages
(1) Accounting Budget Analysis	3
(2) Personnel Budget Analysis	3
(3) Controller's Office	2
(4) Staff Support...............................	2

For Accounting Budget Analysis, package 1 of 3 is the "minimum" work that must be performed if accounting budget analysis work is to be done at all. This level of effort requires two people and could be accomplished *if* supervision could be provided as an *additional* duty of an existing supervisor in the division who is responsible for a different decision unit. Supervision for this activity appears in package level 2 of 3.

Decision Packages 1 of 3 and 2 of 3 together represent the current level of effort. Proposed new activity for 19___ represents an expansion of the current workload and requires additional personnel and funds as depicted in package 3 of 3.

Although package 3 of 3 is considered important by the *Finance Division,* the activity could very well be considered "discretionary" by the Controller and Executive Council. Such a package would be eventually reranked, along with other packages, in priority depicting the relative "value" of the proposed activity *viewed from the Executive Council perspective.*

Managers should not jump to the conclusion that there are *no logical alternatives* to the ways in which activities are currently performed. Each decision unit should be carefully reviewed to determine if more cost-effective alternatives are, in fact, possible.

Instances may be found where it is to the hospital's advantage to *add* personnel in a particular activity and reduce contracted services, particularly when the overall cost to the hospital is reduced, the quality of services is improved on a long-term basis, etc. Conversely, there are also instances where it is to the hospital's advantage to reduce permanent personnel and perform seasonal-type activities using temporary or contracted help. The manager responsible for a decision unit is in the best position to make the required analyses and planning decisions.

Additional Examples:

Additional examples of decision packages prepared for the Finance Division are shown as activities 2, 3, and 4. Alternatives should be *reasonable* and capable of being implemented if necessary. In any case, the implementation of an alternative should result in work output comparable to that performed within the organization at the same level of effort, otherwise the alternative analysis is a waste of time. For instance, a possible alternative to the activity designated "Staff Support—Level 1 of 2" is to drop the activity entirely; for decision package purposes that alternative need not be documented since it may be reached through the *ranking process*.

Note that packages designated 2 of 3 and 3 of 3, for example, are not complete in themselves because they represent *incremental increases* of effort, personnel and dollars over the "minimum" level. The decision package for the Personnel Budget Activity (level 1 of 3) is the minimum; decision package 2 of 3 is the incremental addition to level 1 of 3 required to account for the then current 19ᴬ___ level of activity. Level 3 of 3 is the proposed additional, new effort for 19ᴮ___. The total 19ᴮ___ effort for the Personnel activity is the sum of levels 1 of 3, 2 of 3, and 3 of 3.

Although the examples show fractional personnel counts, it is recommended that packages display only whole people. This may require some reassignment of workloads, for planning purposes only, but it should be obvious that if one package is eliminated in the final ranking and budget-setting process, a fraction of a person will not be dropped from the organization.

When evaluating alternatives, a hospital perspective is adopted, that is, the impact on other departments is assessed when benefits and consequences are being investigated. Only alternatives which are feasible and make good management sense will be pursued.

BF/gl

DECISION PACKAGE

Date   August 25, 19___

ACTIVITY (OR OBJECTIVE) NAME	DEPARTMENT	PREPARED	RANK
Accounting Budget Analysis	Finance		
LEVEL NO. 1 OF 3	DIVISION Accounting	APPROVED	

STATEMENT OF WORK OR PROGRAM

Compile hospital Budget and publish quarterly. Prepare Monthly Operating Reports. Process changes to Budget data base as approved. Process capital equipment budgets.

RESOURCES REQUIRED		CURRENT YEAR	BUDGET YEAR
Personnel		2	2
Labor	$	25,920	28,110
Outside Services	$		
Other	$	960	1,056
Total	$	26,880	29,166

ALTERNATIVE WAYS OF PERFORMING WORK OR PROGRAM AND COSTS

This work could be made an added effort of the Corporate Office. However, unless other work in that office is deleted, additional manning would be required. This and any other alternative would require at least two people.

ADVANTAGES OF RETAINING ACTIVITY

Provides basic administrative support of Budget process. Provides documents for budget decisions by hospital and Board committees.

CONSEQUENCES IF ACTIVITY IS ELIMINATED

It would be impossible for management to develop and approve hospital expenditure proposals in a comprehensive manner. The control of hospital expenditures to assure that timing, magnitude, and need are in balance with other demands on financial resources would be extremely difficult.

DECISION PACKAGE

Date August 25, 19___

ACTIVITY (OR OBJECTIVE) NAME	DEPARTMENT	PREPARED		RANK
Accounting Budget Analysis	Finance			
	DIVISION	APPROVED		
LEVEL NO. **2** OF **3**	Accounting			

STATEMENT OF WORK OR PROGRAM	RESOURCES REQUIRED	CURRENT YEAR	BUDGET YEAR
Supervision of basic effort (level 1). Prepare graphics of Monthly Operating Report. Prepare monthly Budget Variance Report to management, focusing on organizational responsibilities. Develop, with aid of others, improvements to budgeting system. Prepare periodic capital equipment budget variance reports to management.	Personnel	1	1
	Labor $	20,610	22,350
	Outside Services $		
	Other $	480	528
	Total $	21,090	22,878

ALTERNATIVE WAYS OF PERFORMING WORK OR PROGRAM AND COSTS

This, plus level 1 of 3, is the current level of activity. Because supervision and staff work are combined, no lower cost alternative is discernible.

ADVANTAGES OF RETAINING ACTIVITY

Extends budget data beyond basic clerical effort to point where it is digested and displayed for management review of variances so that corrective action may be taken in a timely manner.

CONSEQUENCES IF ACTIVITY IS ELIMINATED

Useful analyses of hospital budget variance, intended for managerial control purposes, will not be available.

DECISION PACKAGE

Date _August 25, 19_____

ACTIVITY (OR OBJECTIVE) NAME	DEPARTMENT	PREPARED	RANK
Accounting Budget Analysis	Finance		
LEVEL NO. 3 OF 3	DIVISION Accounting	APPROVED	

STATEMENT OF WORK OR PROGRAM	RESOURCES REQUIRED	CURRENT YEAR	BUDGET YEAR
Prepare monthly Budget Variance Report to management. Prepare quarterly analyses of proposed revisions to Budget for use by Budget Committee.	Personnel	0	1.3
Devise and implement techniques for screening project proposals.	Labor $	0	21,850
Devise and implement improved staff support to Management Committee in areas involving construction projects.	Outside Services $		
	Other $	0	0
	Total $	0	21,850

ALTERNATIVE WAYS OF PERFORMING WORK OR PROGRAM AND COSTS

None discernible for variance analysis preparation.
Improved techniques for screening project proposals could be devised by an outside consultant for a fee of $5,000 or more.

ADVANTAGES OF RETAINING ACTIVITY

Assist management in exercising the most effective control over expenditures, and balancing considerations of cost and risk, by eliminating marginal projects at the planning/budgeting stage. A conservative estimate of the expected savings is $25,000 per year.

CONSEQUENCES IF ACTIVITY IS ELIMINATED

Existing deficiencies in the hospital and other major projects' planning/budgeting process will not be subjected to critical review and improvement. Hospital may continue to spend at least $100,000 per year needlessly.

DECISION PACKAGE

Date   August 25, 19____

ACTIVITY (OR OBJECTIVE) NAME	DEPARTMENT	PREPARED		RANK
Personnel Budget Analysis	Finance			
LEVEL NO. 1 OF 3	DIVISION Accounting	APPROVED		

STATEMENT OF WORK OR PROGRAM	RESOURCES REQUIRED	CURRENT YEAR	BUDGET YEAR
Compile Personnel and Manpower Budgets and publish annually.	Personnel	1	1
Process approved Personnel and Manpower budget revisions. Prepare Personnel and Manpower budget data for Monthly Operating Report.	Labor $	16,415	17,565
	Outside Services $		
	Other $	480	528
	Total $	16,895	18,093

ALTERNATIVE WAYS OF PERFORMING WORK OR PROGRAM AND COSTS

This work could be made an added effort of the Personnel Department. However, unless other work in that department is deleted, additional manning would be required. This and any other alternative would require at least one person.

ADVANTAGES OF RETAINING ACTIVITY

Provides basic administrative support of hospital Personnel and Manpower Budget process. Provides documents for budget decisions by Finance Committee.

CONSEQUENCES IF ACTIVITY IS ELIMINATED

It would be impossible for management to develop and approve proposals for manpower increases and changes in operating and maintenance expenses on a comprehensive, hospital-wide basis.

DECISION PACKAGE

DEPARTMENT	PREPARED
Finance	
DIVISION	APPROVED
Accounting	

Date   August 25, 19____

ACTIVITY (OR OBJECTIVE) NAME

Personnel Budget Analysis

LEVEL NO. **2** OF **3**

RANK

STATEMENT OF WORK OR PROGRAM

Supervision of Basic Activity (level 1).
Train replacement for Budget Accountant.
Analyze new budget proposals, consult with responsible managers and make recommendations to Management Committee.
Develop and publish budget guidelines, provide training and consultation to managers and budget coordinators in various departments.

RESOURCES REQUIRED		CURRENT YEAR	BUDGET YEAR
Personnel		3	3.6
Labor	$	48,909	58,568
Outside Services	$		
Other	$	3,629	1,584
Total	$	52,538	60,152

ALTERNATIVE WAYS OF PERFORMING WORK OR PROGRAM AND COSTS

This, plus level 1 and 3, is the current level of activity for 19^A____. Because supervision and staff work are combined, no lower cost alternative is discernible. The 0.6 person for 19^B____ represents clerical support to continue present activity while the Clerk is training for the Budget Accountant position. A possible alternative is the retention of a "temporary" on a 3 days per week basis, at an increase in cost of 10%.

ADVANTAGES OF RETAINING ACTIVITY

Extends personnel and manpower proposed budgets beyond clerical compilation. Provides analyses and insights to assist managers and Finance Committee in arriving at prudent budget decisions.

CONSEQUENCES IF ACTIVITY IS ELIMINATED

Useful analyses of personnel and manpower budgets will not be available.

DECISION PACKAGE

Date   August 25, 19____

ACTIVITY (OR OBJECTIVE) NAME	DEPARTMENT	PREPARED		
Personnel Budget Analysis	**Finance**			RANK
	DIVISION	APPROVED		
LEVEL NO. **3** OF **3**	**Accounting**			

STATEMENT OF WORK OR PROGRAM	RESOURCES REQUIRED		CURRENT YEAR	BUDGET YEAR
Seek out and implement improvements in personnel and manpower budgeting and cost control procedures.	Personnel		0	0.8
Prepare monthly variance analysis reports on personnel budgets.	Labor	$	0	15,504
Consult with departments to obtain explanations. Report findings to management in timely manner and encourage corrective action.	Outside Services	$		
	Other	$	0	0
	Total	$	0	15,504

ALTERNATIVE WAYS OF PERFORMING WORK OR PROGRAM AND COSTS

A portion of the compiling work necessary to support the monthly variance analyses could be done on computer. A systems request submitted to Data Processing reveals that such support will not be available until approximately mid-19____. The manpower increase is an analyst; no other lower cost alternative is discernible.

ADVANTAGES OF RETAINING ACTIVITY

Assist management in effecting timely control over personnel expenditures by providing useful variance analysis reports. A conservative estimate of the potential savings in annual expenses is $50,000.

CONSEQUENCES IF ACTIVITY IS ELIMINATED

Existing deficiencies in the personnel and manpower planning/budgeting process will not be subjected to critical review and improvement. Opportunity to save at least $50,000 per year in expenses will be missed due to non-availability of timely variance analysis reports.

DECISION PACKAGE

Date __August 25, 19___

ACTIVITY (OR OBJECTIVE) NAME	DEPARTMENT	PREPARED		RANK
Controller's Office	**Finance**			
	DIVISION	APPROVED		
LEVEL NO. **1** OF **2**	**Accounting**			

STATEMENT OF WORK OR PROGRAM	RESOURCES REQUIRED		CURRENT YEAR	BUDGET YEAR
Provide basic typing and secretarial support to entire Budget Staff.	Personnel		1	1
Provide statistical typing of budget analysis reports.	Labor	$	9,992	11,460
	Outside Services	$		
	Other	$	480	528
	Total	$	10,402	11,988

ALTERNATIVE WAYS OF PERFORMING WORK OR PROGRAM AND COSTS

Share workload for basic typing and secretarial support with another department.
Require one budget accountant or statistical clerk to perform statistical typing as an added duty; retain a "temporary" statistical typist during peak load periods @ $4.00 per hour.

ADVANTAGES OF RETAINING ACTIVITY

Provides fast, accurate typing of reports and correspondence of many kinds. Deadlines for Management Committee meetings are met.

CONSEQUENCES IF ACTIVITY IS ELIMINATED

Productivity of entire department would be seriously impaired. Workload would need to be cut and/or stretched out if deadlines can be pushed out.

DECISION PACKAGE

Date ___August 25, 19___

ACTIVITY (OR OBJECTIVE) NAME	DEPARTMENT	PREPARED		RANK
Controller's Office	**Finance**			
	DIVISION	APPROVED		
LEVEL NO. **2** OF **2**	**Accounting**			

	RESOURCES REQUIRED	CURRENT YEAR	BUDGET YEAR
	Personnel	1	1
	Labor $	27,000	29,160
	Outside Services $		
	Other $	480	528
	Total $	27,480	29,688

STATEMENT OF WORK OR PROGRAM

Provide basic supervision of Budget task.
Provide support and counsel to Budget Committee, Board
Finance Committee, and hospital managers.
Provide technical direction to Budget staff.

ALTERNATIVE WAYS OF PERFORMING WORK OR PROGRAM AND COSTS

No alternative to supervisory responsibility. Support and counsel to committees and managers could be provided by an Assistant Controller, but only at the expense of downgrading or delaying a portion of his existing workload.

ADVANTAGES OF RETAINING ACTIVITY

Provides continuity and leadership to Budget organization.
Provides technical direction for the solution of difficult systems and administrative problems.

CONSEQUENCES IF ACTIVITY IS ELIMINATED

Would cause the hospital budgeting activity to revert to the state that existed prior to the creation of the "Budget Director" position and the change in emphasis which accompanied that action.

DECISION PACKAGE

Date   August 25, 19____

		PREPARED		RANK
DEPARTMENT **Finance**		APPROVED		
DIVISION **Accounting**				

ACTIVITY (OR OBJECTIVE) NAME

Staff Support

LEVEL NO. **1** OF **2**

RESOURCES REQUIRED		CURRENT YEAR	BUDGET YEAR
Personnel		1	1
Labor	$	15,570	22,360
Outside Services	$		
Other	$	360	528
Total	$	15,930	22,888

STATEMENT OF WORK OR PROGRAM

Maintain Budget Division interface with other departments.
Provide consultation and advisory services to other departments concerning budget and accounting data needed to solve problems.
Provide consultation and advisory services to Budget Director.
Provide training instruction to other departments concerning budgeting and cost control.

ALTERNATIVE WAYS OF PERFORMING WORK OR PROGRAM AND COSTS

None discernible.

ADVANTAGES OF RETAINING ACTIVITY

Helps to assure effective utilization of existing budgeting and cost control system. Minimizes costs for modifying existing system or creating new ones by screening change requests for reasonableness.

CONSEQUENCES IF ACTIVITY IS ELIMINATED

Would increase time required by Budget Director, Accounting Analyst and Personnel Budget Analyst to investigate and solve systems problems, conduct training, and interface with Data Processing.

DECISION PACKAGE

ACTIVITY (OR OBJECTIVE) NAME	DEPARTMENT	PREPARED		Date August 25, 19
Staff Support	**Finance**			
LEVEL NO. **2** OF **2**	DIVISION **Accounting**	APPROVED		RANK

STATEMENT OF WORK OR PROGRAM

RESOURCES REQUIRED	CURRENT YEAR	BUDGET YEAR
Personnel	0	0.3
Labor	$ 0	$ 4,705
Outside Services	$	$
Other	$ 0	0
Total	$ 0	4,705

Devise and implement improved staff support to Finance Committee in areas involving financial and economic aspects of Program Plans.

Develop and publish periodic progress and variance and analysis reports on major projects.

Expand training activity as needed to satisfy demands.

ALTERNATIVE WAYS OF PERFORMING WORK OR PROGRAM AND COSTS

Increased manpower for 19____ is estimated at 0.1 man-year of clerical support and 0.2 man-year of analyst support, allocated from other personnel proposed for the Division. Improvements in the planning/budgeting process could be devised by an outside consultant.

ADVANTAGES OF RETAINING ACTIVITY

Assist management in exercising control over projects by eliminating marginal projects in the planning/budgeting process and by providing timely control information for approved projects. A conservative estimate of expected savings is $20,000 per year.

CONSEQUENCES IF ACTIVITY IS ELIMINATED

Existing deficiencies in the project planning/budgeting process will not be subjected to critical review and improvement. Potential savings of $20,000 per year would not be realized.

THE NARRATIVE OF THE DESIGN,
IMPLEMENTATION, AND RESULTS OF THE
ZERO-BASE BUDGETING SYSTEM AT
ALEXIAN BROTHERS MEDICAL CENTER

CASE STUDIES

Table of Contents

PREFACE

The following study* represents the experiences of one of the first hospitals in the country known to implement zero-based budgeting. By its size, location, and other factors, it represents a fairly typical hospital situation and its experiences may be applicable at other institutions.

For reasons identified by the hospital in this study, its zero-based budgeting process had the following specific characteristics and constraints:

1. It was planned as a three-phase implementation with roughly one-third of its total cost centers doing zero-based budgeting each year, over a three-year period, until all departments had implemented ZBB budgets.
2. It initially involved only the personnel components of the budget, representing close to 60 percent of the institution's total operating expenses; it did not include nonpayroll expenses or capital acquisitions.
3. The process was designed for implementation by the Vice President for Operations and his administrative staff rather than by the Vice President for Finance and his fiscal staff.

This study is not intended to serve as an example of how the zero-based budgeting program should be designed and implemented, but rather as an example of the dynamics of implementing this process as this particular hospital designed it for its own needs.

This study reveals some of the actual experiences of administrative officers, financial officers, and departmental managers in designing and implementing the first phase with 21 departments over an 18-month period. These experiences give some insight into the following critical questions and issues:

1. What kind and degree of commitment by the Board of Trustees, administration, and middle management was obtained and was this sufficient to make the zero-based budgeting process viable?
2. What is the relationship between the institution's administrative organization and the effectiveness of implementing zero-based budgets in this particular study?
3. What is the relationship between the hospital's preexisting incremental budgeting process? Namely: is a transition to zero-based

---

*Portions of this report have been excerpted from *Hospital Financial Management*, September 1978, "How One Hospital Applied Zero-Based Budgeting (and Won)" by Dean E. Grant and Bruce Fisher.

budgeting a dramatic change in budgeting preparation and implementation? Are incremental and zero-based budgeting complementary to each other in any meaningful ways?

4. Can zero-based budgeting be applied to certain departments while retaining incremental budgeting in other departments or should it be applied to all departments for greatest effectiveness?

5. What are the most common ploys utilized by middle managers to prevent undesired trade-off decisions by administration?

6. What are the most common problems faced by administration in making trade-off decisions and in ensuring effective follow-through by middle management? Of special relevance in this particular study is the corollary issue of the hazards of delegating these trade-off decisions to too low a level in the organization?

7. Can zero-based budgeting work effectively when applied only to manpower budgeting and not to other operating expenses and equipment decisions?

8. How does the zero-based budgeting process relate to other critical functions of the hospital, including the planning process, personnel systems, management engineering, etc?

I. BACKGROUND

Alexian Brothers Medical Center is a 407 bed not-for-profit Catholic community hospital in the Northwest suburbs of Chicago. The Medical Center has 1300 employees (representing 1100 Full Time Equivalents) and operates on a $30 million budget. Its fiscal year is the calendar year and its annual budgeting process begins in late August and culminates in final acceptance by the Board of Trustees in early December. The Board of Trustees has an active Finance Subcommittee which oversees the budgeting process. Alexian Brothers Medical Center has a detailed, formalized budgeting process that integrates closely with the annual One Year Plan of the Medical Center. In this latter process, the Medical Center's Five Year Plan is revised and updated annually, and by early August, the Board of Trustees and its Planning Subcommittee approve the specific objectives and plans for the upcoming year. This is then presented to the managers, department heads, nursing supervisors, and head nurses so they can begin formulating their own annual objectives in relation to the institution's overall objectives, and this, in turn, becomes the basis for their initial departmental budget presentations to their appropriate administrative officers in late August. The administrative officers (assistant administrators or division directors) then have to make some tough trade-off decisions, representing the priorities and needs of the Medical Center for the upcoming fiscal year.

II. WHY ZERO-BASED BUDGETING AT ALEXIAN BROTHERS MEDICAL CENTER?

A critical aspect of this budgeting process, like most traditional hospital budgeting, is the fact the managers tend to relate their budget requests to new programs and services for the upcoming year. Traditionally, the administrative staff, in turn, devotes most of its energies to evaluating the validity and need for a new program or service and the resources requested to introduce or expand these services, as presented by the managers. In other words, everyone in the budgeting process seems to be concentrating their efforts on justifying or challenging new expansion requests. As commendable as this is, it still leaves a lot to be desired and the current concerns about hospital cost containment, together with the recent interest in zero-based budgeting, as promulgated by the Carter administration during his tenure as governor of Georgia, helped our Board and administrators realize what might be lacking in our traditional budgeting process. Namely, it appears that managers and administrators focus their budgeting efforts on expansion, rather than consolidation and cutbacks, because the whole hospital industry has been focusing its energies on expanding and adding new technologies and services, so the traditional budgeting process can, at best, only provide a means for trading off which of 10 or 20 new expansions or major capital purchases should take place in the upcoming year.

Again, there is nothing inherently wrong with the hospital industry and its management trying to be responsive to new, more effective diagnostic and therapeutic technologies and the ever-increasing public demand for better and broader ranged services. The problem, however, is that we tend to keep adding and adding, and not subtracting obsolete personnel and expenditures. Or perhaps more correctly, it could be said that we are more logical and methodical in our decisions to add a new program or service to our budget than we are when we should phase one out. An example: Many years ago when Basal Metabolism Rates were obsoleted by new, more effective procedures, we simply ceased providing this procedure at our hospital and left it up to the manager to determine how best to reallocate her staff who used to perform these procedures in some other more useful ways. This reallocation of a .5 FTE technician did not receive the same administrative scrutiny and justification as when the position had been requested originally, because it never surfaced as part of the budgeting process per se.

Our traditional budgeting process is designed to very effectively handle only that which is being asked for ... and doesn't come to grips with what isn't asked for or with what is assumed to be necessary. If, like in the above Basal Metabolism Rates example, you can assume that in the last ten years many other new technologies (and new technical specialists) have been added and many others have been obsoleted, you could guess that there are many employees in our system who are probably performing new roles that were not specifically budgeted for and justified. This is not to imply that managers convert these into featherbedding positions. In fact, there is no question that good middle managers will typically convert or re-allocate such positions and functions to other useful purposes in their own departments which, in fact, may make their departments operate more smoothly or effectively. The point, however, is that this was not a decision formally approved by administration as part of the budgeting process, nor was it made available to other competing needs of the organization beyond that one department.

More important perhaps than the consequences of obsolete positions due to changing technologies, is the fact that health care priorities are con-tinually changing, while the total financial resources for health care are gradually becoming more constrained. For example, in the last several years there has been a very major planning thrust by government and in-surance carriers in the areas of ambulatory care and efforts to reduce duplication of acute care beds and major capital expenditures. This may mean that hospital administration may have to think about approving 10 FTEs at $100,000 for a new ambulatory care department and not approve a request for 8 more RNs to open four more inpatient beds—or perhaps to budget $50,000 to staff a new planning department at the expense of some other existing department. Again, traditional budgeting doesn't really help too much in these kinds of trade-offs. Let's say the Board realizes it needs to hire a planning director and an assistant (to relate effectively to the new local Health Systems Agencies and the State Planning Boards) and rather than increase room rates or charges beyond 9 percent-10 percent, the Board may direct administration to choose some other department or de-partments to cut back on to capture this $50,000. However, the way de-partment heads present their budgets, it is virtually impossible to deter-mine which departments could afford this kind of cutback in staffing or operating expenses. Their budgets are presented to defend what they already have or to defend what more they want for the new fiscal year.

For these reasons, we decided that our institution might benefit significantly by zero-based budgeting. Not only would it show up some positions that were never formally approved relative to their present functions, but it would require the manager to justify each position of his department against the overall objectives and purpose of his department. This kind of detailed evaluation would allow administration to make more logical trade-offs, as for example, when the need for $50,000 for a planning department staff might be found by reducing one educational coordinator (with a known consequence for this decision) and a reduction of one employee health nurse (also with a known consequence for this trade-off). Zero-based budgeting was, therefore, perceived by us as a management tool that would not only relate fiscal planning to disciplined management by objectives, but would also allow us to reevaluate all past formal and informal resource allocation decisions against present priorities.

In summary, then there are basically two general reasons why Alexian Brothers Medical Center opted to implement zero-based budgeting.

1. The new cost containment thrust and the need to tighten up on total operating expenses required us to look not just at the trade-offs for the upcoming budget year, but to review all functions of all employees and departments in the entire system to determine which non-critical or obsolete positions have been carried in our existing budget; and to reevaluate these in light of present cost constraints and present institutional priorities so, if appropriate, they can be eliminated or reallocated to areas of current high priority.
2. The dynamics of the whole health care system in the 1970s and the consequent need to more effectively plan institutional objectives and commitments (in light of P.L. 93-641 and H.S.A. efforts) also warranted the development of a system that would allow administration to easily assess the need for staffing additions or reductions in various different departments of the Medical Center as our own corporate plans and objectives changed from year to year. In other words, the more information administration had on each department, its functions, its employees' roles, etc., the better our position to make effective and timely staffing trade-offs when required by changes in the One Year Plan or the Five Year Plan.

III. DESIGNING THE ZERO-BASED BUDGETING PROCESS FOR IMPLEMENTATION

With these general purposes in mind, we proceeded to design a way to implement zero-based budgeting at Alexian Brothers Medical Center. The following were key considerations:

1. We were aware that zero-based budgeting was a new concept and may be perceived by some of our middle managers as just another temporary pop management concept that would fade away if ignored or resisted.

2. If the concept was misinterpreted by middle managers or misapplied by administration, it might end up as a mechanism for pushing off the responsibility for making undesirable cuts and trade-offs to lower level management.

3. By its very name, we guessed "zero-based budgeting" might be perceived as threatening to our middle management; it apparently implied that none of the positions you presently have are approved anymore and your whole department might be wiped out by this new management tool.

4. Likewise, we guessed middle management might perceive it as an impossible task ... especially for a manager with 60 employees, or a $400,000 annual expense budget, to have to justify every existing position or expenditure would initially seem like a half a year of budget preparations.

5. We also expected some managers (and administrative staff) to resent the hospital's financial officers—being deeply involved in evaluating their operational needs. In other words, zero-based budgeting might be perceived as too "financial" in its orientation or that this new effort was an indication that the hospital was becoming controlled by profit and loss considerations only—impressions we did not intend or want to convey by implementing zero-based budgeting. Our institution's existing incremental budgeting process had well established the key line relationship between managers and their respective administrative officers and we had to ensure that the implementation of zero-based budgeting didn't change this by putting the financial staff in a position of having to make trade-off decisions.

6. We were also aware that unless administration successfully convinced and reassured the middle managers that this was a process that would ultimately benefit them rather than penalize them, they would make the zero-based budgeting output impossible to evaluate and utilize for any trade-off decisions. We also had studied some of

the literature relative to zero-based budgeting and were able to anticipate some of the more common ruses to make zero-based budgeting ineffectual, e.g. one resisting tactic is for the department head to offer up essential functions as low priority items, knowing full well that administration wouldn't seriously consider cutting these, and, thereby, taking attention off high priority ranked items which are not so essential.

7. We also concluded that if we made any drastic and major trade-off decisions too quickly, based on their zero-based budgeting presentations, we would discourage middle management's future participation in this kind of process, or at least make it significantly more difficult to obtain their positive commitment in the future.

8. We had time limits and limited administrative employee relations and finance department staff resources to devote to a full scale effort in 19___, and we, therefore, had to focus our efforts in those areas that would give us both a good trial experience and also some likelihood of real benefits.

9. For our first trial of the zero-based budget concept, we decided to focus only on employee complements. Not only would this allow a concentrated effort in this area, but for this whole process to work at all, it was necessary to have a very clear understanding of each department's roles and functions, and this, in turn, should relate to the roles, responsibilities and duties of all of its employees from the Department Head on down. It is not really possible to begin evaluating each function or activity within a department until this process is completed; only then can priority rankings be done. At our institution we had already begun the process of reevaluating and rewriting all existing 250 job descriptions (in relation to a new merit review process we had recently implemented), so our Employee Relations Director was in an ideal position to assist the participating managers in putting together their zero-based budgeting presentations. All final zero-based budgeting presentations had to include current job descriptions for all employees in their department and departmental activities had to be tied back to every employee of the department. If a hospital does not have current, written job descriptions for all its employees, the zero-based budgeting process would be a very difficult task.

A second reason for concentrating our trial efforts on employee complements was that there is more comparative information available in this area. H.A.S. reports and productivity standards are available for virtually all classifications of employees. This information not only helped us determine which areas to look for the greatest benefits of zero-based budgeting (i.e., the greatest possible overstaffings), but will also allow us to evaluate more easily the consequences of zero-based budgeting efforts.

10. In addition, to focus our efforts in those areas that might yield tangible benefits, we looked for those departments and divisions where some or all the following conditions existed or might exist:

   (a) Those departments that tend to have an overlapping of functions to one extent or another, on the theory that such departments are more likely to have duplicative staffing worthy of an administrative review that might not have been obvious in past years' traditional budgeting reviews. Engineering and Housekeeping Departments sometimes have these overlaps—so too, even Physical Therapy and Occupational Therapy Departments. Central Supply and the Operating Rooms also sometimes have functional overlapping, especially in the areas of sterilization and supply. Social Service, Patient Accounts and Pastoral Care Departments also tend to have some overlapping functions.

   (b) All departments where major new programs or services or new classifications of personnel had been established in the last five years; the theory here was that when a new program or concept is introduced, it is often not immediately known what other departments or employees will be impacted or even obsoleted by this change. By the time a major new program is fully absorbed into the system, all the shock waves within the rest of the department or on other departments seem to go unnoticed unless it results in requests for more employees; i.e., no one seems to voluntarily report excess staffing they now have as a consequence of the change ... only increased needs for staffing will, with certainty, be reported. For example, the introduction of "Clinical Nurse Specialists" partially obsoleted the Head Nurse's role, plus partially obsoleted some other functionalized support staff, e.g. the dietitian, social worker, etc.

   Or the introduction of a decentralized medical records technician program (putting ARTs directly on the nursing units) may obsolete some of the functions of the unit clerk, staff nurses and other staff. Changing from a team concept of nursing care to a modular or primary care program can have similar effects on a wide variety of remotely related employees. One could even conjecture that the more major and innovative a new program is, or the longer it takes to be effectively absorbed into the system, the greater the likelihood that obsolete positions will develop and not be detected as part of the traditional budgeting process.

(c) Those departments that have not had a change in the manager/ director in at least the last seven years, on the theory that some miniempires might have been gradually built up; it is recognized that even the best of managers might be reluctant to volunteer up positions he had fought for eight years ago, but which are no longer so critical to the department or hospital as they once were.

Incidentally, it should be added that we didn't opt to exclude revenue producing departments from our selection of departments to begin the first phase of zero-based budgeting. In fact, quite the contrary—several of these departments were specifically selected because they were revenue-producers. Although it is often assumed that these types of departments don't carry any more fat than necessary (presumably because they are miniprofit centers where new costs are only approved if they are exceeded by new revenues), it is more likely that the opposite is true and that zero-based budgeting of these areas would be beneficial. In traditional incremental budgeting, these department heads frequently use the following line: "If you want more revenue and, therefore, more profit from our department, we have to have this new FTE." This usually convinces the administrator and no further questions are asked. What should be asked, but usually isn't: can't we increase our profit ratio even more by not increasing our staffing and still handle the increased volume. Also, because most states don't have rate review commissions, revenue producing departments can typically raise their charges and increase their profits without any relationship to improved productivity or efficiency. In other words, these departments historically have been subjected to less budgeting scrutiny than nonrevenue producing service departments and, therefore, are ideal for zero-based budgeting.

11. We were aware that effective objective-setting by departments can't take place until higher level objectives, including Board and administration, were established and clear. Fortunately, our institution had developed a long range plan two years ago and each year revised and updated this plan via the formulation of a One Year Plan (similar to an H.S.A. "Annual Implementation Plan"). Therefore, we were in an ideal position to share with the participating managers the upcoming proposed One Year Plan against which they could relate or develop their own departmental objectives. Though prob-

ably not an impossible task, it certainly would have been significantly more difficult to implement an effective, meaningful zero-based budgeting process if such a plan were not available.

12. Finally, we recognized there would be inherent limitations in not programming zero-based budgeting in all departments of the Medical Center—a price we had to pay for trying to implement a first phase on relatively short notice. Since many departments have overlapping or partially overlapping functions with other departments, it would have been ideal to be in a position to easily compare the zero-based budgeting presentations of all such departments, and either eliminate unnecessary duplication or concentrate activities in one rather than several departments. But perhaps a more important deficiency in this phased approach is that, in the absence of zero-based budgets simultaneously presented by all departments, it is impossible for higher level administrative officers to consolidate all decision packages of all departments and consequently impossible to create a single comprehensive ranking of the lower level rankings from all 100 cost centers. The best we would be able to do is a final aggregate ranking of the rankings from only 29 cost centers in the first year.

For example, it is quite possible that even the lowest ranked function of one department may be more critical to the institution than the second or third highest ranked function of another department, but unless both such departments are zero-based budgeted, the higher level institutional ranking can't be done effectively.

In spite of this potential serious deficiency in the phased approach to zero-based budgeting, we decided to do it this way for the following reasons. First, as noted earlier, for the sake of expediency; that is, having one-third of the departments on zero-based budgets was better than none, especially if this effort didn't compromise the long range benefits of zero-based budgeting. Secondly, we felt the quality of zero-based budgeting output in a limited number of areas would be greater than what we could expect from all 100 cost centers, simply because of the extraordinary amount of time involved by managers and administrators to develop these. And finally, if the zero-based budgeting budgets were properly done they would have validity well beyond a one-year or two-year horizon, unlike incremental budgets. After all, a zero-based budget should be exactly what it implies—it assumes starting from zero with a logic for each function and resource allocated above zero. Thus, even though our phased approach would not allow the highest level ranking institutionwide in its first year, by the beginning of the third year it would be possible to do so because the zero-based budgets that were developed in the first and second years would still be basically valid. Incidentally, as a corollary to this, it could be argued that zero-based budgeting each year would only yield marginal benefits and that a good zero-based budget is probably viable for five years.

IV. IMPLEMENTATION

Given the above considerations, the following steps were taken:

Administration, and specifically the Vice President of Operations, was identified as the initiator of the zero-based budgeting program, rather than having the Vice President of Finance and the Controller perceived as the program initiators and coordinators. Middle managers were advised that this was to be a management process rather than a financial process and that they would be required to proceed with their traditional budget efforts simultaneous with their zero-based budgeting efforts. This not only reduced some of the anxiety about this potentially being a complete budget slashing of the entire department, but also lessened the potential threat of "financial officers" making decisions about operational matters in their departments.

To make this new process a less than major burden, we focused on only 29 cost centers rather than all 100 centers, and also restricted it to staffing only, rather than nonpayroll operating expenses and capital. This helped the participating middle managers to concentrate their efforts in the most important area—their staffing—which represented roughly 60 percent of their annual expenses. The selection of only 29 cost centers was important because (a) it allowed a restricted, controlled trial and (b) it was consistent with administrative and financial staff time that was available to direct the development of these budgets. How these 21 departments (representing 29 cost centers) were selected was also critical. It was important that middle management did not perceive this first phase to be aimed at those departments suspected of being "overstaffed" or "poorly run", which could only have resulted in resentment and ultimately resistance at being singled out. It was also important to have a roughly equal distribution of departments under each of the three assistant administrators, lest the middle managers conclude that one division had more serious problems than the other two divisions.

In spite of the above concerns, we did, in fact, select several departments that we suspected might not be efficiently staffed. To identify these departments objectively, we compared all department's staff complements with their counterparts at other neighboring hospitals and also with the regional Hospital Administrative Services (H.A.S.) data for hospitals our size. Department heads were not advised that their departments appeared over or understaffed by comparison with their counterparts because we didn't want to elicit any hyperdefensive (or alternatively lax) behavior on their part as they developed their zero-based budgeting presentations. We also specifically included four department heads who were new to their jobs, i.e., who had been appointed department heads in the last 12 months. The reason for this was that we suspected these individuals might be more willing to identify and admit excess or inappropriate staffing as they weren't responsible for budgeting these excesses in the past. Finally, as noted above, we included several departments in the final selection that appeared to be well run and efficient, so it would not appear anyone was being picked on for a specific purpose.

For the first year's phase of implementation, the following 21 departments (representing 29 cost centers because some departments have subsections) were selected: Pharmacy, Central Distribution, Materials Management, Biomedical Engineering, Dietary, Housekeeping, Social Service, Laboratory (Chemistry and Hematology sections only), Radiology, Physical Therapy, Occupational Therapy, Respiratory Care, Outpatient Department, EKG, Operating Room, Recovery Room, Rehabilitation Medicine Unit (Nursing), Alcohol Treatment Unit (Nursing), Mental Health Unit (Nursing), and two Medical/Surgical Units. The first seven departments above fall under the Division Director for Support Services; the next seven departments come under the Division Director for Professional Services, and the remaining seven departments/units come under the Division Director for Nursing Services. Incidentally, this selection of departments, in effect, resulted in zero-based budgeting being applied to 478 FTEs out of our total complement of 1,100 FTEs—159 FTEs in the Support Services Division, 204 FTEs in the Nursing Service Division, and 115 FTEs in the Professional Services Division.

Since this first year's efforts only involved slightly more than a third of all department heads, managers, and head nurses, we had to make sure that these middle managers perceived this as a positive, useful process, so next year the other middle managers would be open and willing to participate positively. It was also important that we not initiate any major cutbacks in quick response to their zero-based budgeting presentations. We deliberately decided to wait at least four months after budgets were submitted before meeting with the middle managers to talk about the very complex and sensitive trade-offs or possible reductions. In this way, it would be perceived as an administrative review, not necessarily tied to their budget efforts, and therefore, reduce the possibility of the zero-based budgeting process being misperceived as punitive.

The administrative staff (consisting of three assistant administrators, employee relations director, planning director, public relations director, controller, medical director, two Vice Presidents and the President) were all coached on the process and potential pitfalls. Their full understanding and support was gained so their middle managers would perceive the whole process as a meaningful exercise. A detailed format was worked up by the Vice President of Finance, so there would be consistency in the application and end products, in spite of the fact that each manager was to deal with his own administrative officer. As in our traditional budgeting process, the managers were expected to make their presentations to only their immediate administrative officer, rather than to a committee or a more senior administrator or financial officer.

The following detailed steps, protocol, and forms were given to each of the three Division Directors to be distributed and discussed with their department heads. These steps, as stated below, can be viewed as instructions directly to the department heads by administration:

Step 1: Prior to starting your zero-based budget, you should list the objectives and activities you wish to accomplish in 19____. These objectives/activities should be listed in numerical order in the priority you establish using Exhibit A.

Step 2: In order to accomplish your objectives, and to maintain fundamental activities, your present departmental organizational chart should be reviewed and revised if necessary. The organizational chart should depict your department in a functional approach. Names are not to be used, but the number of full-time equivalents by function is required.

Step 3: To ensure that your present organization and distribution of manpower in your department can be effectively related to departmental activities and objectives, you will need to review each job description of each employee in your department (and if necessary propose revisions to your administrative officer and then Employee Relations Director if some position descriptions are no longer consistent with departmental tasks or activities).

Step 4: After review and approval of Steps 1-3 above by your appropriate administrative officer, you should designate each cost center in your department (if you have more than one) as a "decision unit" and proceed to develop all the decision packages for this cost center or decision unit.

Step 5: Determine which are appropriate "decision packages" for each cost center and analyze these. This step is the crux of the operational planning activity. It results in a series of succinct, documented decisions concerning the activities to be performed in the budget year. Each decision package should provide sufficient information concerning a continuing or planned activity to permit you and your administrative officer to reach agreement as to whether: the activity should be continued or eliminated, continued at the same level of effort or modified, continued to be performed in the same manner, or be replaced by a more cost-effective alternative. The selection of departmental basic "activities" and "objectives" is the basis for each decision package and each activity or objective should be evaluated in terms of the level of effort involved to achieve. Level 1 should represent the minimum level of effort and resources required; that is, below the current level of effort. Level 2 should approximate the current level of effort for this activity or the proposed level of effort necessary to fulfill this objective. Level 3 or more should represent additional levels of effort required to improve on this activity or objective.

Step 6: Complete Decision Package (Exhibit C) using detailed instructions in Exhibit B.

Step 7: Evaluation and ranking of decision packages:

This involves an assessment of the relative priorities of all activities and objectives proposed to be performed during the budget year. The prioritization is performed initially by the manager responsible for the budget. Subsequently, it is reviewed with his administrative officer and various adjustments are agreed to. As part of the review and evaluation process, low priority packages are screened by the administrative officer for departments under his jurisdiction to determine possible trade-offs among departments and reprioritization of the more discretionary items. Finally, the ranking forms and low priority decision packages are presented to the Vice President of Operations and Vice President of Finance for discussion, evaluation of relative merits on a hospitalwide basis, and finally, determination of lowest priorities and total budget level for each department.

At the department level where the plan and budget originate, the responsible manager should rank all the activities he is responsible for in 1-2-3 order, from highest to lowest priority.

He can do this by simply sorting the decision packages like a deck of cards and then placing a priority number on each page in sequence. If he wishes, he can instead use a "weighting system" to quantify the relative merits of a decision package. Two problem areas should be avoided during the review and ranking process:

1. Managers should not concentrate their time on activities that are legally or operationally required (other than to ensure that all alternatives, cost reduction opportunities, and operating improvements have been explored and incorporated as appropriate), but should concentrate on discretionary activities.

2. Managers should not spend too much time worrying whether activity 4 is more important than activity 5, but only assure themselves that activities 4 and 5 are more important than activity 15, and activity 15 more important than 25, etc. *See Exhibit D for instructions on completing the Priority Rank Form (Exhibit E).*

In summary then, the following steps occurred.

The decision packages are first developed by the department heads (with input from their appropriate supervisors or head nurses). These decision packages (numbering in excess of 150 for the 29 cost centers) included a detailed listing of the departmental objectives for the upcoming year plus all job descriptions of all employees in the department, in relationship to each function performed by the department. Within each decision package, the department head ranked each activity, function, or objective by a level he considered appropriate; for example, "level 1 of 5" levels of activity indicated this was the most basic and fundamental activity of this particular department or section, while "level 5 of 5" indicated the least basic function of the department. For each level of activity a detailed listing of all its components was included, as well as a summary of specific costs required to provide this service or level of activity. In addition, each decision package included the department head's statement of suggested alternative ways of providing this service, advantages of retaining this service or function, and consequences if eliminated.

Once completed, these decision packages were submitted to the next highest level, the division directors. At this level, the division director had to review several things, including: whether the department head's own statements of departmental objectives are consistent with the objectives of that entire division as interpreted by the division director; whether the appropriate levels of activity or functions of the department are properly identified and, if so, whether the relative position of these levels appears to be consistent with the department's overall objectives; whether the costs assigned to each level are reasonably correct; whether the department head's statement of alternative ways of meeting these objectives or fulfilling these functions is adequate; and whether the statement of advantages of retaining this activity or function versus the consequences of eliminating it is sufficiently analyzed; and finally, whether the department head's own ranking of all levels in his decision package is reasonable.

Since approximately only a third of the cost centers under each division director were zero-based budgeted in this first year's phase, the division directors were not expected to formally consolidate revised rankings of the decision packages from all their areas. Instead, they were expected to take account of the functional rankings or priorities of those departments who did zero-based budgeting and, where possible, work with those department heads to explore possible implementation of some of the most cost-efficient alternatives of providing specific levels of service. Where the only alternative offered was the elimination of an existing service, the division director was required to obtain approval, before proceeding with this, from the Vice President of Operations. In this sense, then, we would be able to begin utilizing the zero-based budgeting results from 29 cost centers, even though we would have to wait until the third year before we would have zero-based budgets from all areas and, therefore, could not immediately do a consolidated ranking and revised ranking at each successive level of the organization for all decision packages.

Finally, it should be pointed out that this implementation process followed our existing organizational lines. ... As in our routine incremental budgeting process, all budget requests filter up from the department heads (or patient care coordinators for nursing) to their appropriate administrative officer who, in turn, makes an evaluation of all such middle management requests in relationship to the needs and objectives of his or her entire Division. Following this level of evaluation, the budgets are submitted to the Vice President for Operations who, in turn, evaluates all requests in relationship to the needs of all internal operating areas and does so in consultation with the Director of Personnel, the Vice President of Finance, and the Controller. Finally, the operational budgets along with the budget requests from the Vice President of Finance and the Medical Director are submitted to the President/C.E.O. who makes a complete organizationwide assessment of needs and priorities before submitting these budgets (whether zero-based or incremental) to the Board of Trustees.

ALEXIAN BROTHERS MEDICAL CENTER ORGANIZATIONAL CHART

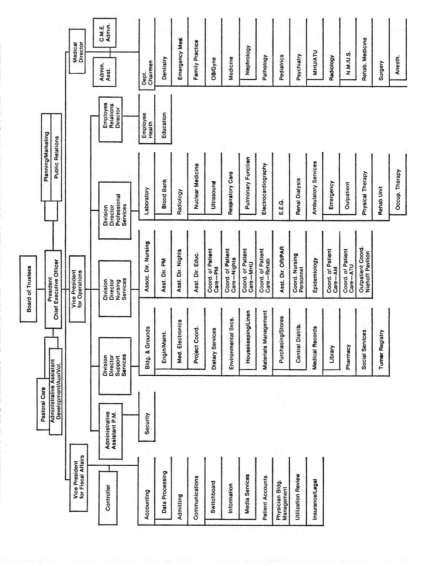

V. RESULTS

Several predictable things have occurred as a result of the implementation of the zero-based budgeting trial at Alexian Brothers Medical Center ... and some surprising things also happened. The surprises first.

First, contrary to our expectations, every one of the 21 managers became fully committed and enthusiastic about being asked to participate, within one week of starting their preparations. It is possible that this might relate to the old "Hawthorne halo effect" whereby employees' interest and commitment tend to increase simply because they are participating and being observed in a trial situation or special program. More likely, however, is the fact that the middle managers obtained some personal satisfaction in developing these types of budgets. This was the first time some of these managers had been given direction in the formulation of "management by objectives" plans and budgets. They spent a great deal of time reviewing every job description in their department and attempting to relate these to: the functions performed by the department, the objectives of the department, and the broader objectives of the Medical Center. Some zero-based budgeting presentations were so thorough and detailed in their evaluations and explanations that the final packets ran in excess of 50 pages. In reading these and discussing them with the managers, we got the very distinct impression that the managers were very proud of their output and that, in a sense, they had fully satisfied themselves that their departments were efficient and functionally effective in relation to the organizational objectives.

An interesting corollary to this was that the assistant administrators received the most thorough budget presentations they had ever received and the many questions and probes that administration typically asks of managers during traditional budget presentations simply weren't appropriate ... virtually all the questions were already anticipated and answered in the presentations. A typical Housekeeping budget presentation used to require about three to four hours' time for administrative review and clarification with the department head—for the employee complement portion alone. With zero-based budgeting, this required only about a half-hour before the assistant administrator ran out of probing questions. What had, in fact, happened in this process was that managers had come to think more like administrators as they developed their budgets, and in a sense, partially obsoleted some aspects of the traditional role of an assistant administrator in the budgeting review process. The presentations were simply too good to be challenged in any meaningful way and the assistant administrators were very quickly faced with the trade-off decisions. And even when it came to trade-off decisions, the middle managers had already answered what alternatives could be considered and what would be the likely consequences if a particular activity were eliminated. The format used specifically asked the middle manager three key questions that normally administrators ask at the budget review: What alternative ways are there for performing these tasks? What advantages are there in retaining this or that activity? And, what would be the consequences for the Medical Center if this or that activity by your department were eliminated?

Although the middle management response was extremely positive, the quality of the zero-based budget packages was uneven in some respects. First, we noted that the decision packages from the Nursing Service Division varied dramatically from the format it was supposed to use. In fact, the Nursing zero-based budgeting decision packages will not lend themselves to a higher level ranking review and all but three of these Nursing cost centers will be required to develop zero-based budgets again next year. Upon further investigation, it appears that there are at least four reasons why the Nursing Division produced such poor results compared with the other two divisions. First, the Division Director apparently wanted to encourage flexibility in her head nurses and supervisors in developing their zero-based budgets and did not insist on strict adherence to the established formats. It is likely that these nursing supervisors did not really understand the process as they would have if they had been required to follow the format. Second, the internal organization of the Nursing department is quite different from the other two divisions and reporting lines and lines of accountability for budgeting and administrative decision making are relatively less clear. Third, in this previous fiscal year, the Nursing Division as a whole had suffered from serious understaffing and apparently many of the head nurses and supervisors perceived "zero-based budgeting" as an opportunity to prove definitively that they were in dire need of dramatic increases in staffing just to provide the most basic nursing services. Finally, according to the Division Director of Nursing Services, her impression was that these head nurses and supervisors simply could not identify any functions that were in their opinion less than absolutely essential.

As could be predicted, the most sophisticated managers produced the highest quality decision packages. However, we also found several ruses used in even the best packages. Some of these are as follows:

1. Some low level, noncritical activities appeared with high level rankings, perhaps because the department head had a special interest or bias in favor of this activity and didn't want it scrutinized as a low ranked level. An example: In the final rankings by the Social Service

Director, he ranked 3 of 3 (the lowest level of level 3) as his Number 1 departmental priority. As it turns out, "level 3 of 3" was tied to his request for a second departmental secretary, and by no stretch of the imagination could we see how another secretary was more important than providing basic professional social service functions.

2. Some packages appeared to be totally lacking in reasonable "alternatives" for the existing function or activity. More specifically, some decision packages stated alternatives in such a way that it made the department head look good for the way he was providing this service; also some alternatives were stated so that the alternative appeared so difficult or costly as not to be taken seriously. In other cases, the alternative was to simply transfer a part or all the function to another department (with no apparent efficiencies to be obtained). And in other cases, it was simply suggested that the activity be performed by an external contract, typically without any cost estimates of what this contract might cost.

   For example, one of the alternatives for the Building and Grounds Department to provide landscaping services was simply "contract it out", without any detailed estimates of this cost. Another so-called alternative that frequently was offered was "computerize the function". The above-listed examples of noncreative alternatives and pseudoalternatives were easily handled by the administrative officer. In fact, this is one area that the administrative officer, together with the department head, can really work together on to generate more viable and more creative options once the functions have been clearly articulated.

3. Likewise for the sections of the decision package that required a statement of advantages of retaining the activity, and consequences if the activity were eliminated. For example, some diversionary tactics: "Revenue will be reduced unless this activity is retained", "Quality of care will be compromised", "Turnaround time will increase" (without any quantification), "Lost or late charges might result", "Violation of existing hospital policies", "Loss in quality control", and so on.

The zero-based budgets from those 21 departments (or 29 cost centers) generated 156 decision packages (not even including the 7 nursing cost centers which didn't use the same formats) and this, in turn, resulted in 484 separate levels of activity to be ranked. In the support services alone, this required the Division Director to evaluate almost 300 levels of activity, and again, this was representative of only a third of the cost centers in that division. Incidentally, all department heads were advised that level 1 of an activity had to be interpreted as the most basic level of activity to accomplish the purpose of that particular function; level 2 had to represent what the department currently performed relative to that activity and level 3 represented what more might be required to more effectively accomplish that task. Levels higher than 3 represented additional improvements in the particular activity that were desirable.

The general consensus of all managers who participated in zero-based budgeting was that the most difficult part of the whole process was the final ranking phase. All but two of the seven nursing cost centers couldn't even generate rankings at all, because they perceived all their functions of equal and critical importance. Some department heads had to turn to their immediate administrative officer for help in the ranking process. In the end, we found that most departments utilized a ranking process similar to the one shown in Case Example G, and a few used the type shown in Case Example F.

For the reasons that will become clearer in Case Example A, the administrative staff had an even harder time of reranking the zero-based budgeting decision packages from their areas, although they were not specifically required to finalize these rankings because about 60 percent of their departments had not done zero-based budgeting, and it would be unfair to force trade-off decisions in only those departments that had participated in zero-based budgeting, while not likewise seeking trade-offs in the nonzero-based budgeting departments.

In spite of several problems that occurred in this final phase of implementing the first year's zero-based budgeting, the administrative staff did realize some major benefits. The following table summarizes all FTE reductions or trade-offs that resulted from this process, classified under several categories that we found were the apparent source of the savings.

Finally, our administrative staff cited the following real benefits (pros) and problems (cons) with the zero-based budgeting process as we had implemented it:

Pros:

1. It gave even greater structure to our already well-structured budgeting process, thereby streamlining the whole process for both the department heads and administrative officers.
2. Zero-based budgeting gave the Division Directors (i.e., assistant administrators) and the Vice President for Operations an extremely thorough and deep understanding of the intricacies of the operations of their various departments. All three Division Directors felt they were now significantly more knowledgeable about the inner workings

of their departments, their objectives and interrelationships with other departments.

3. In a similar vein, the department heads themselves felt they had a better understanding of their own departments, their priorities, and necessary resources to achieve their objectives.

4. Due to zero-based budgeting, the administrative staff felt that the department heads had finally begun to think more along "management by objective" lines and had learned the importance of integrating specific job descriptions with specific tasks in their departments. At least one department (Operating Room) decided to revise two of its key job descriptions, as a consequence of zero-based budgeting, when it was discovered that the positions did not properly reflect tasks they were expected to perform in the department.

5. Most managers (with the notable exception of Nursing managers) came to realize that not all activities of their department have equal importance, even though most department heads did, in fact, have difficulty in the ranking process.

6. In several areas, interesting and potentially very viable alternatives were generated that have warranted further in-depth study ... alternatives that otherwise might not have surfaced up from the department heads if they had not been working with the structured zero-based budgeting decision package formats.

Cons:

1. Time-consuming for the managers and extraordinary amount of paper was generated.

2. Administrative officers were faced with an almost unmanageable number of rankings, even though only a third of their areas were zero-base budgeted. As noted earlier, the Division Director for Support Services was faced with almost 300 separate levels of activity to rank. If all departments had participated in zero-based budgeting, it certainly would have been necessary to apply an arbitrary 70 percent or so cutoff factor to keep this manageable.

3. Inconsistent application of the process in the three Divisions, with the Nursing Division not even consistently using the same format, caused the Vice President of Operations and Vice President of Finance difficulty in comparing and coordinating the decision packages.

4. Possible misuse of the process by administration (see Case Example A) and misunderstanding of the process by department heads (see Case Examples B and C).

SUMMARY OF STAFF REDUCTIONS THROUGH ZERO-BASED BUDGETING ALEXIAN BROTHERS MEDICAL CENTER

(Based on 29 cost centers representing 156 decision packages and involving 478 FTEs)

Factor	Action
1. Obsolete positions due to: 1.1 Changes in technologies causing obsolescence	EKG Tech .5 FTE eliminated from EKG budget (carryover from elimination of BMR in 1972)
1.2 New program/service implemented without determination of consequential obsolescence of positions elsewhere after program/service fully implemented	See Case E .25 FTE—Social Service
1.3 Position obsoleted by change in institutional or departmental priorities	1.9 FTE Respiratory Care—equipment cleaning
2. Duplicative position or duplicative functions	See Case Example D .6 FTE Security. Also consolidating transportation team—1.0
3. Elimination of existing service deemed no longer critical	None to date
4. Elimination by more efficient option of contracting out for service	None to date
5. Elimination of positions via determination of ghost functions (i.e., Department not really performing a particular function as stated)	See Case Example C .4 FTE Social Service
6. Other—miscellaneous	9.1 FTEs eliminated See Case Example A
Total	13.75 FTEs eliminated

CASE EXAMPLE A

In Section III (Evaluate and Rank All Decision Packages) we made reference in No. 2 to the inherent danger of using the zero-based budgeting process as a means of pushing off undesirable trade-off decisions to lower levels. Even though we were well aware of this and had hoped not to abuse the process this way, this unfortunately did occur to some extent. What is critical about this case example is how easily this happens and what consequences occur when it is allowed to happen. (As the Vice President for Operations, I will attempt to clarify how I inadvertently sanctioned this.) When all 150 decision packages were submitted, the packages appeared to contain an extraordinary amount of valuable information that might have allowed the respective Division Directors to easily identify overlapping functions, obsolete positions, and low priority activities that could be eliminated. These 150 packages had over 400 levels of detailed activity that could be subjected to review and informal reranking. From my point of view, as Vice President of Operations, the detail in these packages was so exhaustive that I simply could not evaluate it. The department heads clearly had a good understanding of their operations and the resources they considered necessary to perform their functions and I felt that, if properly used, the appropriate assistant administrator/division director had a very valuable tool to look for F.T.E. savings or cutbacks.

Therefore, rather than requiring reranking by each of the three Division Directors of all their zero-based budgeted departments, I implicitly allowed them to prioritize the trade-offs they could find in these decision packages, to give them a target to strive for, and also to test the zero-based budgeting process. They were asked if they felt they could reduce their upcoming fiscal year budget requests (which they had already cut significantly before submitting them to me) by approximately 50 percent; this, however, was not a mandate but rather a query about this potential. The Support Service and Professional Service Division Directors decided they felt they could, while the Division Director for Nursing felt she could not because her seven zero-based budget areas had not provided adequate ranking information to allow this. The two other divisions had requested seven and 14 new FTEs, respectively, in the final budget requests for the upcoming fiscal year and, therefore, agreed to utilize the zero-based budgets to bring this down to a net addition of 4 FTEs and 7 FTEs. A very critical point, however, is that as Vice President of Operations I advised them that based on expansion of services and the addition of new programs, their original aggregate request of 21 specific new FTEs was approved, i.e., all these positions were justified. However, the net approved figure would only be 11 FTEs and with the use of their zero-based budgets in conjunction with the department heads, they were to try to find areas to reduce from existing operations or services that would give them the 10 new positions they wanted.

In this sense, the burden of effectively utilizing the zero-based budgeting results was put on these two Division Directors because we had no other way to perform higher level rankings of all packages from all areas (i.e., all 100 cost centers).

What happened next was a further compounding of the problem when, in fact, the Division Directors also implicitly allowed the department heads to establish their own priorities for eliminating existing FTEs rather than working closely with the department heads to evaluate which positions could be eliminated without compromising essential services of the hospital or without compromising the performance of other departments. As noted in some of the following Case Examples, the problems this caused were serious, even though the end result was a net FTE saving of in excess of 13. It should be pointed out, however, that the Division Directors didn't simply mandate reductions of each zero-base budgeted area, but rather advised these department heads that a certain number of positions, in aggregate, were being sought and that their support in helping identify noncritical functions to phase out was requested.

CASE EXAMPLE B

One of the most interesting experiences during the implementation of zero-based budgeting occurred several months after the new fiscal year had begun when our Director of Pharmacy found his inpatient pharmacy staff drastically overburdened with an unanticipated long duration of exceptionally high inpatient census. After having apparently utilized other options, including increasing overtime coverage, temporary expansion of part-time pharmacy positions to full time, vacation recalls, and so on, he turned to his original zero-based budgeting proposal and found what he considered his only solution in an area he had previously articulated as a function of only intermediate level priority. This function was the provision of outpatient pharmacy services from 9 A.M. to 10 P.M. daily, largely to fill emergency patients' prescriptions, outpatient prescriptions, and all discharged inpatient prescriptions.

In his original zero-based budgeting presentation he had listed as an alternative to providing this outpatient service, its elimination as such, with the main inpatient pharmacy assuming some of these duties when necessary. His immediate administrative officer, the Division Director for Support Services, had not requested that he proceed with this trade-off of services, but in the absence of this administrative officer from the hospital at the peak of this exceptionally high demand on the inpatient pharmacy (due to high census), this Director of Pharmacy took the initiative on his own to proceed with this particular alternative; that is, temporarily closing down the outpatient pharmacy service and redirecting this freed-up staff to the inpatient pharmacy. Needless to say within an hour of this action, the Vice President of Operations interceded with a mandate to reopen the outpatient pharmacy as this was an unacceptable trade-off that affected the workloads of several other departments (including Nursing Services and Emergency Services) without having fully explored other trade-off options within the pharmacy itself.

This example demonstrates several relevant issues. First, even though this department head correctly wanted to concentrate his resources into the area which represented his department's most critical objectives and highest priorities, what appeared to him to be implementation of an alternative that was solely within his province (i.e., within the Pharmacy as a whole), in fact had ramifications in other departments and divisions of the Medical Center and should have had administrative sanction and, if necessary, coordination, to lessen the impact on other areas. Apparently the Director of Pharmacy had come to believe that he had the right to exercise virtually any of the alternatives he had listed in his original zero-based budgeting package.

This underscores one of the basic problems with our zero-based budgeting process. We specifically chose not to finalize the zero-based budgeting rankings and institute all possible trade-offs and cutoffs immediately after the time of the presentations. Instead, we opted to keep the process fluid so that, if and when necessary, the appropriate administrative officer and his department head could reevaluate the zero-based budget decision packages during the year and make trade-offs and cutoffs as appropriate.

Zero-based budgeting by its nature is a dynamic process and requires a phasing of implementation of alternatives throughout the year as these alternatives are fully explored and coordinated and as the need for restricted staffing and expenditures may become manifested. However, the consequence of not having resolved all these issues at the front end is that we may have left some basically unacceptable rankings and alternatives in the zero-based budgeting decision packages, and the department heads may feel that since specific alternatives haven't been rejected, or specific rankings by the department head weren't revised, they may be viable and implementable alternatives and acceptable rankings of functions.

As noted in Case Example A, a very real possible explanation for why this happened was that this department head's immediate administrative officer (the Division Director) may have pushed the decision making relative to the alternatives down to the department head level and, thereby, mistakenly sanctioned the Department Head to make the trade-off decisions on his own. After the dust settled, the Director of Pharmacy insisted that his administrative officer wouldn't make a decision so he had to act, while the Division Director contended that he was attempting to find a better solution.

Another and perhaps more interesting issue in this particular example is that the Director of Pharmacy may have been turning to zero-based budgeting "alternatives" long before such dramatic trade-offs were really necessary. In this sense, he may have been using his zero-based budgeting process as a substitute for routine management problem solving. For example, even though the inpatient pharmacy demands were excessive and were taxing his staff, it didn't happen overnight. The census had been steadily rising for the previous four weeks and other routine management options could have been anticipated, short of a sudden decision to completely close down the outpatient pharmacy. It is also certainly not beyond questioning whether the most dramatic zero-based budgeting alternative was chosen by this department head as the solution, with the possible intent of making administration acutely aware of the extreme workload on the Pharmacy staff.

CASE EXAMPLE C

As approximately only one-third of all the hospital's cost centers participated in zero-based budgeting in the first year of the three-year phased implementation, we faced the problem of trying to evaluate some departmental zero-based budgeting presentations in relationship to other departments that didn't participate in this first year. Probably one of the best examples of this potential problem occurred in the relationship between the Social Service Department and the Patient Accounts Department. The former was involved in zero-based budgeting while the latter department did incremental budgeting and was programmed for a later implementation of zero-based budgeting. The key issue that surfaced here had to do with whether the Social Service Department was, in fact, really involved in patient financial counseling, as stated in their decision package; and what exactly was their role versus the Patient Accounts Department and what priority did this task have in Social Service as compared with the priority Patient Accounts would have given it. Without having the Patient Accounts Department on zero-based budgeting, it was difficult to determine to what extent and with what priority they perceived this to be their role.

As it turned out for three social worker positions (out of seven FTE social workers in the department), this task was ranked at level 2 out of the 3 levels available. And in each case, the suggested alternative way of performing this task was simply "financial counseling could be handled by the Business Office (i.e., Patient Accounts)". In addition, the task called "financial counseling to patients" was itself too nebulous to really allow the administrative officer for this area to get a real fix on what this entailed. Did it, for example, mean that the social worker "counseled" the patient by simply referring him or her to the Patient Accounts Department for more detailed assistance, or did it involve a detailed financial assessment of the patient followed by a determination by the social worker of public aid funds (or other resources) that might be available to the patient and assistance in applying for such?

During the zero-based budgeting presentations, the Director of Social Services insisted that his social workers were very deeply involved in all aspects of financial counseling, including assistance in filing applications for financial assistance when appropriate. The only way to clarify this, without having a zero-based budgeting presentation from the Patient Accounts Department, was to begin a line of inquiry directly with the Director of Patient Accounts. The first step was to call for the job description of this department's Public Aid Coordinator, which quickly revealed that several financial counseling functions were apparently part of this individual's responsibility. Based on this, the Public Aid Coordinator was called in with the Director of Patient Accounts and they were asked to review the decision packages that had been submitted by the Director of Social Services. They were somewhat disturbed to see that the Social Service Department was taking credit for this financial counseling task when, in their opinion, these three social workers merely referred potential financial hardship cases to the Public Aid Coordinator. In addition, it was pointed out to us that this function could probably be better and more efficiently handled by the social workers rather than the Public Aid Coordinator because these three social workers (assigned to the mental health, alcohol treatment, and rehabilitation medicine units) were required to get a very comprehensive social history on these types of patients and in the process establish a good understanding and rapport with these patients, who otherwise might resent or resist the suggestion that they apply for state or county financial assistance (even if they could qualify). In addition, it was pointed out that the social workers have to make a preliminary financial determination of the eligibility of all patients admitted to these three units for funding coverage by various special agencies, e.g. Department of Mental Health grants to the Medical Center for care to eligible patients.

After this input was obtained, it was necessary for the administrative officer who was responsible for the Social Service Department (who was different from the administrative officer who was responsible for the Patient Accounts Department), to meet and discuss with the Social Service Director the apparent overlapping or duplication of functions. The point of this example is that several additional administrative steps were involved to sort this out, whereas a simple comparison of the Social Service and Patient Accounts zero-based budgeting presentations would have quickly revealed this potential duplication of tasks.

So what ultimately happened in this case? The administrative officer responsible for Social Service (i.e., the Division Director for Support Services) quickly found himself in a serious confrontation with the Director of Social Service when he challenged the time and FTE allocations related to "financial counseling". An interesting side effect of this zero-based budgeting generated confrontation was that it forced the Social Service Director to articulate for the first time his professional philosophy that social workers shouldn't really get involved in any financial counseling, which was something the Division Director obviously had not been aware of. The Social Service Director remained adamant that he would not require his social workers to get deeply involved in financial counseling even if it would allow a reduction of manpower in the Patient Accounts Department, and this untenable position warranted intervention by the Vice President of Operations and the Vice President of Finance (to whom the Patient Accounts Department reports) and the final decision was made that the Social Service Department would, in fact, get deeply involved in all public aid financial evaluations and referrals for patients on these three specialty units. This effectively reduced the Public Aid Coordinator's role from a full time 1.0 FTE position to approximately .6 FTE and reinstituted a true financial counseling task to the social workers.

Stepping back a bit further to see what this example means in a broader perspective, it is quite clear what apparently had happened and how this institution had gradually absorbed an unnecessary extra .4 FTE. The Director of Social Services apparently had evolved a professional philosophy (that had gone unchallenged until now, because it had never been clearly articulated) that social work shouldn't include financial counseling any longer. The Public Aid Coordinator's position gradually grew in responsibility to fill the void being left by Social Service, but the scope of the responsibilities of the social workers was not simultaneously reduced via their job descriptions to reflect that they weren't really devoting any time to financial counseling and referrals. Since our zero-based budgeting process requires a one-to-one correspondence between all tasks or "statements of work" performed by the department and the specific job duties of each individual in the department (as defined in the official job descriptions), the Director of Social Service apparently felt obliged to include in his departmental objectives and departmental tasks the role of financial counseling, and consequently exposed this declared statement of work output to a test. In this sense, zero-based budgeting, even though only a partial first ·phase implementation, helped surface up a highly vulnerable ghost function.

CASE EXAMPLE D

As might be expected, those tasks the department head had always considered a burden or a nuisance for his department were often the very tasks to be suggested in the decision packages for another department to assume under the "alternative" section. For example, Nursing Services was quick to suggest other departments (e.g. Physical Therapy, X-Ray, EEG, etc.), could handle patient transport or dietary tray removals, etc. Typically, though, it was hard to get a good fix on the number of FTEs, if any, that would be offered with this transfer of tasks. Worse, though, was the fact that nonzero-based budgeting department heads weren't really in as strong a position to resist the proposed transfer of duties to them without correspondingly adequate staff transfers to support this, simply because their own budgeting process was less structured and they generally weren't even aware that some other department head was developing a detailed proposal that involved the alternative of a transfer of duties to that department.

An example of this occurred when the Materials Manager made the assumption (which eventually turned out to be correct) in his zero-based budgeting presentation for the Motor Pool Section that he could reduce his drivers' required manhours for interhospital and intersatellite transport by having evening and weekend security officers man the shuttle bus in the nonpeak demand hours of service. The Security Department had done a routine incremental budget and did not anticipate this alternative proposal coming forth from the Materials Management Department. Incidentally, the reason this ultimately worked out well—with the Security Department accepting this duty and the Materials Management Department saving almost .5 of an FTE in its motorpool by this transfer of duties alternative— was not because the Security Department was overstaffed, but rather because the actual time commitment for driving the bus between the hospital and its satellite was not significant. However, because the service is critical when required, the Motor Service Pool had to provide off-hour standby staffing. In this sense, this example also represents another kind of situation that zero-based budgeting helped surface up for scrutiny and higher level trade-offs; namely, the problem of inefficient standby staffing that can sometimes be ameliorated by utilizing more versatile and cross-trained staff as an effective alternative.

CASE EXAMPLE E

Our Mental Health Unit Supervisor and Head Nurse were included in the zero-based budgeting program, as was our Social Service Department, which includes two social workers specifically allocated to the Mental Health Unit. In the Mental Health Unit zero-based budgeting presentation by the nursing supervisor and head nurse, they pointed out that their present primary care nursing organization allows each patient's primary care nurse to directly "coordinate care with other disciplines and ensure that the patient is followed up by other appropriate health facilities or providers after discharge". An avenue worthy of exploration then was to evaluate what role the psychiatric social workers perceived relative to post-discharge follow-up of such patients, as distinguished from the role of the primary care nurses.

The zero-based budgeting presentation relative to the psychiatric social workers' roles stated that they were to "provide discharge planning services for patients who may require placement in other follow-up facilities" and "to provide referral service information".

It was interesting to note that even though both the Mental Health Unit primary care nursing staff and the psychiatric social workers felt they had a responsibility in effective discharge planning to "assure continuity of services that were started in the MHU", neither zero-based budgeting presentation offered this function as a possible trade-off or alternative reallocation of responsibility to the other department. In pursuing this further, it became apparent that the three Mental Health Unit Nursing Team Coordinators (to whom the primary care staff nurses report) each spend about three hours each week (or nine hours total) directing discharge planning efforts and follow-up arrangements for their assigned patients.

This nine-hour per-week time allocation, plus another hour by the primary care nurse herself, may not seem like a whole lot to consider trading off (or reducing) from Social Service. However, it does seem to point out what is probably happening in small pieces, but large in aggregate, throughout the entire system; namely, when our Mental Health Unit was developed eight years ago, its nursing organization was designed on the functional and team concept, and the need for two social workers was probably legitimate, i.e., nursing wasn't expected to ensure follow-through, post-discharge, with its patients. When primary care was introduced a few years ago, the social workers were not cut back, probably because the new, broader role of the primary care nurse wasn't well articulated at that time, and also probably because it simply wasn't considered reasonable to cut back each of two existing 40-hour social worker positions to 35 hours per week.

CASE EXAMPLE F

Following are three pages that represent the Final Priority Ranking sheets prepared by the Director of Pharmacy. It is interesting to note how his ranking of his 10 decision packages consisting of 33 levels of activity differs from the approach taken by the department head in Case Example G. From administration's point of view, both types of rankings are consistent with the process as it was designed, but the pharmacy example shows an interesting approach of incorporating real alternatives as separate decision packages right back into the ranking process. What this case example basically says is that the first-ranked activities (No's 1-15) are more critical to the fulfillment of the pharmacy objectives than No's 15-33 and that no cutoffs of 1-15 can be tolerated. However, it does not say that the top-ranked items are what we are currently doing, but rather what we must do if we are to continue to meet even the most basic objectives of the department.

Therefore, as a matter of fact, the item ranked No. 1, "Traditional system with 16 hours of service", is significantly less than what we presently provide; namely, our current level is the one that appears as ranking No. 16. So, too, No. 4 "No billing" is a step less than what we currently do in the area of billing (i.e., No. 6) and, therefore, represents the absolute minimum for this particular activity. By "no billing" he was suggesting an option he didn't even favor, but ranked it high as a minimal, necessary option; that is, incorporate a fixed amount into the hospital rooms representing average pharmacy charges per patient and cease separate charging by the pharmacy. Overall this ranking, therefore, does not represent what the department head wants or thinks is good, but rather is ranked in order of what is needed (including undesired alternatives) as basic to the operations of the department.

PRIORITY RANKING

Date September 1, 19____

DEPARTMENT	DIVISION
Pharmacy	Support Services

PREPARED	
Department Head XXX	
APPROVED	
Division Director YYY	PAGE 1 OF 3

RANK	ACTIVITY NAME AND DESCRIPTION	LEVEL NO.	NO. OF NO.	CURRENT YEAR PER-SONNEL	$ (000)	BUDGET YEAR PER-SONNEL	$ (000)	CUMULA-TIVE $ (000)
1	Traditional System with 16-hour service.	1	6	8.0	128,900	8.0	140,500	140,500
2	No I.V. Additive Program with distribution of additives through the Drug Distribution System.	1	3	0.0		0.0		140,500
3	Alcohol Control with perpetual inventory (legal requirement), narcotic control without perpetual inventory.	1	3	1.4	15,026	1.4	16,378	156,878
4	No billing. Pharmacy charge incorporated into the patient room rate.	1	4	0.0		0.0		156,878
5	Director.	1	3	0.0		0.0		156,878
6	Billing of requisitions (traditional and unit dose systems).	2	4	1.4	15,026	1.4	16,378	173,256
7	Alcohol and narcotic perpetual inventory control.	2	3	0.0		0.0		173,256
8	Clerical functions handled by the Pharmacy administrative level.	1	3	0.0		0.0		173,256
9	Pharmacy clerk handling the clerical functions.	2	2	0.0		0.0		173,256
10	Maintenance and upkeep of pharmaceutical library.	1	5	0.0		0.0		173,256
11	Take-home prescriptions filled by the traditional system.	1	2	0.8	12,888	0.8	14,050	187,306
	TOTALS							

PRIORITY RANKING

DEPARTMENT	DIVISION	PREPARED
Pharmacy	Support Services	Department Head XXX
		APPROVED
		Division Director YYY

Date September 1, 19____

PAGE 2 OF 3

ACTIVITY			CURRENT YEAR		BUDGET YEAR		
RANK	NAME AND DESCRIPTION	LEVEL NO. OF NO.	PER-SONNEL	$ (000)	PER-SONNEL	$ (000)	CUMULA-TIVE $ (000)
12	Secretary handling clerical functions.	3 / 3	1.0	11,606	1.0	12,651	199,957
13	Director with Assistant.	2 / 3	1.0	27,331	1.0	29,790	229,747
14	Traditional System with 24-hour service.	2 / 6	2.0	32,222	2.0	35,122	264,869
15	Unit Dose System with 16-hour service.	3 / 6	1.0	10,732	1.0	11,698	276,567
16	Unit Dose System with 24-hour service.	4 / 6	1.0	10,732	1.0	11,698	288,265
17	I.V. Additive Program with 24-hour service.	2 / 3	1.0	21,489	2.0	35,122	323,387
18	Addition of Staff Supervisors.	3 / 3	2.2	50,794	2.2	55,365	378,752
19	Employees' prescriptions filled by the traditional system.	1 / 2	0.3	6,447	0.3	7,027	385,779
20	Outpatient and Emergency Room medications filled by the traditional system.	1 / 2	0.4	8,596	0.4	9,370	395,149
21	Computerized Drug Distribution with 24-hour service.	5 / 6	0.0		0.0		395,149
22	Computerized I.V. Additive Program with 24-hour service.	3 / 3	0.0		0.0		395,149
	TOTALS						

PRIORITY RANKING

Date September 1, 19____

DEPARTMENT	DIVISION
Pharmacy	Support Services

PREPARED	
Department Head XXX	PAGE 3
APPROVED	OF 3
Division Director YYY	

	ACTIVITY		CURRENT YEAR		BUDGET YEAR		
RANK	NAME AND DESCRIPTION	LEVEL NO. OF NO.	PER-SONNEL	$ (000)	PER-SONNEL	$ (000)	CUMULA-TIVE $ (000)
23	Computerized billing generated from Pharmacy input.	3 of 4	0.0		-1.4	-16,378	378,771
24	Computerized perpetual inventory control.	3 of 3	0.0		0.0		378,771
25	Computerized filling of take-home medications.	2 of 2	0.0		0.0		378,771
26	Computerized filling of employee medications.	2 of 2	0.0		0.0		378,771
27	Computerized filling of outpatient and Emergency Room medications.	2 of 2	0.0		0.0		378,771
28	Technician educational training program.	2 of 5	0.0		0.0		378,771
29	I.V. drug administration lectures to nursing personnel.	3 of 5	1.0	21,490	1.0	23,425	402,196
30	Rotating pharmacists to the nursing units for review of charts.	4 of 5	0.0		0.0		402,196
31	Computerized billing generated from charting of medications at the time of administration.	4 of 4	0.0		0.0		402,196
32	Computerized Drug Distribution with 24-hour service with Pharmacy technician on nursing units.	6 of 6	...		...		402,196
33	Consumer orientation of disease states.	5 of 5	...		...		402,196
TOTALS			22.50	373,279	22.10	402,196	402,196

CASE EXAMPLE G

Unlike Case Example F, the Director of Central Distribution consistently ranked all her basic level activities highest (i.e., level 1 appears in the first 11 rankings) and current level activities as the next most important in the ranking (i.e., level 2 appears ranked from 12-22) while her lowest rankings are applied to levels 4, 5 and 6. What this basically says is that she feels that all of her basic functions (a) must be retained and (b) there are no other viable alternatives to substitute for these basic activities. The same logic was applied to levels 2, 3, 4 and 5.

What is important about this Case Example versus Case Example F is that even though both are acceptable ways of ranking, it can be difficult for the next level, Division Director, to apply a 65 percent or 70 percent cutoff rule to these two departments and get consistent and comparable rankings.

PRIORITY RANKING

DEPARTMENT	DIVISION	PREPARED	
Central Distribution	Support Services	Department Head XXX	PAGE 1
		APPROVED	OF 4
		Division Director YYY	Date October 6, 19___

	ACTIVITY	LEVEL		CURRENT YEAR		BUDGET YEAR		
RANK	NAME AND DESCRIPTION	NO.	OF NO.	PER-SONNEL	$ (000)	PER-SONNEL	$ (000)	CUMULA-TIVE $ (000)
1	Administration—Supervisor.	1	3	1	19,720	1	21,490	21,490
2	Processing trays & instruments—items sent to units upon request.	1	5	.5	4,745	.5	5,170	26,660
3	Sterilization steam or ETO—department only.	1	5	.5	4,745	.5	5,170	31,830
4	Aeration for ETO—room aeration.	1	2	.5	5,170	.5	5,170	37,000
5	Equipment—delivery upon request.	1	3	.5	4,745	.5	5,170	42,170
6	Cleaning and maintenance of area—work areas cleaned frequently.	1	5	.2	1,896	.2	2,170	44,340
7	Clinical & educational—writing of procedure.	1	4	.3	5,736	.3	6,447	50,787
8	Supply distribution—department not involved. Supply dispensed per case from stores.	1	4	0	0	0	0	50,787
9	Billing process—no billing, central distribution charges incorporated in patient room rate.	1	3	.2	1,896	.2	2,170	52,957
10	Linen preparation—department trays & reverse isolation linen.	1	4	.1	947	.1	1,034	53,991
11	Secretarial—clerical functions per central distribution supervisor.	1	3	0	0	0	0	53,991
	TOTALS							53,991

PRIORITY RANKING

DEPARTMENT	DIVISION
Central Distribution	Support Services

PREPARED	
Department Head XXX	
APPROVED	
Division Director YYY	

Date __October 6, 19___

PAGE 2 OF 4

RANK	ACTIVITY NAME AND DESCRIPTION	LEVEL NO. OF NO.		CURRENT YEAR PER-SONNEL	CURRENT YEAR $ (000)	BUDGET YEAR PER-SONNEL	BUDGET YEAR $ (000)	BUDGET YEAR CUMULATIVE $ (000)
12	Processing trays & instruments—additional units stored on unit.	2	5	.1	940	.1	1,034	55,025
13	Sterilization steam or ETO—smaller units.	2	5	.5	4,745	.5	5,170	60,195
14	Equipment—some units store for use.	2	3	0	0	0	0	60,195
15	Cleaning and maintenance of area—shelf and drawer areas cleaned.	2	5	.1	948	.1	1,085	61,280
16	Clinical & educational—attaining of education book.	2	4	0	0	0	0	61,280
17	Supply distribution—distribution per requisition to patient or unit.	2	3	4	37,960	3.5	36,190	97,470
18	Billing process—manual charges written on requisition and interdepartmental charge.	2	4	1.8	17,082	1.8	18,612	116,082
19	Linen preparation—preparation & procedure for small usage department including st. for surgery.	2	3	.1	949	.1	1,034	117,116
20	Secretarial—central distribution typing clerk did functions.	2	3	.5	4,745	.5	5,170	122,286
21	Administration—technician I and II.	2	3	.4	3,796	.4	4,130	126,416
22	Aeration for ETO—mechanical aeration.	2	2	0	0	0	0	126,416
TOTALS								126,416

PRIORITY RANKING

Date   October 6, 19____

DEPARTMENT	DIVISION
Central Distribution	Support Services

PREPARED	Department Head XXX
APPROVED	Division Director YYY

PAGE 3 OF 4

RANK	ACTIVITY — NAME AND DESCRIPTION	LEVEL NO.	OF NO.	CURRENT YEAR PERSONNEL	CURRENT YEAR $ (000)	BUDGET YEAR PERSONNEL	BUDGET YEAR $ (000)	CUMULATIVE $ (000)
23	Processing trays & instruments—preparation of instruments and trays.	3	5	.4	3,805	.4	4,131	130,547
24	Sterilization steam or ETO—surgical and labor & delivery.	3	5	1.5	14,235	1.5	15,510	146,057
25	Equipment—supply areas besides nursing units.	3	3	0	0	0	0	146,057
26	Cleaning and maintenance of area—exchange cart and autoclave carts washed monthly.	3	5	.2	1,896	.2	2,170	148,227
27	Clinical & educational—development of education program.	3	4	.2	1,898	.2	2,068	150,295
28	Supply distribution—distribution per exchange cart and requisitions.	3	3	(1.2)	23,725	(1.2)	20,690	170,985
29	Billing process—comp. inpatient billing manual departmental charge billing.	3	4	(1)	(9,490)	(1)	(10,340)	160,645
30	Linen preparation—preparation & processing linen packs for surgery and labor & delivery.	3	3	1.8	17,082	2.3	23,782	184,427
31	Secretarial—secretary performs functions.	3	3	0	0	0	0	184,427
32	Administration—supervision by function.	3	3	0	0	0	0	184,427
33	Processing trays & instruments—preparation of instruments and trays for labor & delivery.	4	5	0	0	0	0	184,427
TOTALS								184,427

PRIORITY RANKING

Date __October 6, 19___

DEPARTMENT	DIVISION	PREPARED
Central Distribution	Support Services	Department Head XXX
		APPROVED
		Division Director YYY

PAGE 4 OF 4

RANK	ACTIVITY — NAME AND DESCRIPTION	LEVEL NO.	NO. OF NO.	CURRENT YEAR PER-SONNEL	CURRENT YEAR $ (000)	BUDGET YEAR PER-SONNEL	BUDGET YEAR $ (000)	CUMULATIVE $ (000)
34	Sterilization steam or ETO—case cart labor & delivery.	4	5	0	0	0	0	184.427
35	Cleaning and maintenance of area—cart washer for weekly processing.	4	5	0	0	0	0	184.427
36	Clinical & educational—development of wider training program and follow-up.	4	4	0	0	0	0	184.427
37	Billing process—comp. patient and unit billing.	4	4	0	0	0	0	184.427
38	Processing trays & instruments—preparation of instruments & trays for surgery.	5	5	0	0	0	0	184.427
39	Sterilization Steam or ETO—case cart surgery.	5	5	0	0	0	0	184.427
40	Cleaning and maintenance of area—case carts frequently used.	5	5	0	0	0	0	184.427
TOTALS				13.2	173.914	13.2	184.427	184.427

CASE EXAMPLE H—A COMPLETE DECISION PACKAGE

This is a simple example of how one cost center (Home Care Division of the Social Service Department) developed its 19____ Departmental Objectives/Activities Form (equivalent to Exhibit A) and how it developed its Decision Package (equivalent to Exhibit C). In the final Priority Ranking Form for all sections of the Social Service Department, 18 levels of activity were ranked and the three levels of home care services were ranked as the 6th, 12th, and 17th.

ALEXIAN BROTHERS MEDICAL CENTER

Department Name: Social Service (Home Care)   19___ Departmental Objectives/Activities

(1) Provide discharge planning services for all patients needing follow-up care at home.

(2) Provide information and referral services to inpatients.

(3) Provide information and referral services to employees and members of the community.

(4) Coordinate Meals-on-Wheels Program.

(5) Coordinate School Physical Program.

(6) Liaison with American Cancer Society—Reach to Recovery and Ostomy Visitation Programs.

(7) Hospital and community planning and coordination through Continuity of Care Coordinators Assn., Elk Grove Coordination of Services Committee, Social Service Department meetings, Discharge Planning Committee, Early Rehab Team, etc.

(8) Liaison with Utilization Review Dept. (daily)

(9) Home Care services to all diabetic patients.

(10) Assist in the development of a Home Health Aid Program.

(11) Assist in the development of Home Care portion of the HOSPICE Program.

(12) Liaison with Cook and Du Page County Health Departments and all private community home care services.

(13) Provide all service providers with written discharge summaries as well as physician's orders for continued care.

(14) Assist in patient teaching.

(15) Provide orientation to hospital staff and physician regarding Home Care services.

(16)

DECISION PACKAGE

Date September 2, 19____

ACTIVITY (OR OBJECTIVE) NAME	DEPARTMENT	PREPARED	RANK
Home Care	Social Service	Department Head XXX	6
LEVEL NO. 1 OF 3	DIVISION Home Care	APPROVED Division Director YYY	

STATEMENT OF WORK OR PROGRAM	RESOURCES REQUIRED		CURRENT YEAR	BUDGET YEAR
Discharge planning services for patients needing follow-up care at home.	Personnel		.5	.5
Information and referral for inpatients.				
American Cancer Society liaison—Reach to Recovery, Ostomy Visitation.	Labor	$	6,895.20	8,894.80
Meals-on-Wheels.	Outside Services	$		
School Physical Program.				
	Other	$		
	Total	$	6,895.20	8,894.80

ALTERNATIVE WAYS OF PERFORMING WORK OR PROGRAM AND COSTS

Turn school physical program over to Nursing.
Assign Meals-on-Wheels liaison to another worker in the Social Service Department.
Discharge planning services—no feasible alternative.

ADVANTAGES OF RETAINING ACTIVITY

Provides patients and their physicians well-rounded continuity of care when patient is going home after discharge.
School physical program and Meals-on-Wheels Program provide community services needed in the local area.
Information and referral services to inpatients bring the expertise of a specialist in Home Care services to our inpatients.

CONSEQUENCES IF ACTIVITY IS ELIMINATED

Lack of adequate discharge planning for those patients needing follow-up care at home.
Lack of appropriate liaison with Meals-on-Wheels Program resulting in inefficient follow-up for patients requiring this service.

DECISION PACKAGE

ACTIVITY (OR OBJECTIVE) NAME	DEPARTMENT	PREPARED		RANK
	Social Service	Department Head XXX		12
Home Care	DIVISION	APPROVED		
LEVEL NO. 2 OF 3	Home Care	Division Director YYY		

Date September 2, 19____

STATEMENT OF WORK OR PROGRAM	RESOURCES REQUIRED		CURRENT YEAR	BUDGET YEAR
Information and referral to employees and community people. Departmental liaison with Utilization Review Department. (daily)	Personnel		.5	.5
Services to diabetic patients.	Labor	$	6,895.20	8,894.80
Coordination with inhospital and community through Continuity of Care Coordinators Association, Elk Grove Coordination of Services Committee, Social Service Dept., Discharge Planning Committee, Utilization Review Committee Early Rehab Committee.	Outside Services	$		
	Other	$		
	Total	$	6,895.20	8,894.80

ALTERNATIVE WAYS OF PERFORMING WORK OR PROGRAM AND COSTS
No alternative for information referral other than to drop community information and referral component and let the Employee Assistance Program pick up the service to employees.
Liaison with American Cancer Society must be handled by one person. It could conceivably be handled by someone within Nursing who is given that responsibility and freedom to casefind throughout the hospital.

ADVANTAGES OF RETAINING ACTIVITY
This plus level 1 provides a basic level of service. Basically, these activities ensure that the Home Care Program will be integrated with all programs of the Medical Center.

CONSEQUENCES IF ACTIVITY IS ELIMINATED
Loss of public relations and tangible health to employees and people in the community.
Lack of effective follow-through with cancer patients who require Reach to Recovery and Ostomy visitors.
Lack of total integration of the Home Care component of the programs to the Medical Center.

DECISION PACKAGE

Date September 2, 19 _____

ACTIVITY (OR OBJECTIVE) NAME	DEPARTMENT	PREPARED	RANK
Home Care	Social Service	Department Head XXX	17
LEVEL NO. 3 OF 3	DIVISION Home Care	APPROVED Division Director YYY	

STATEMENT OF WORK OR PROGRAM

Develop Home Health Aid Program in conjunction with Nursing Education.
Develop Home Care portion of HOSPICE Program in conjunction with Administration.

RESOURCES REQUIRED	CURRENT YEAR	BUDGET YEAR
Personnel		
Labor	$	
Outside Services	$	
Other	$	
Total	$	

ALTERNATIVE WAYS OF PERFORMING WORK OR PROGRAM AND COSTS

Home Health Aid Program could be done exclusively by the Nursing Education Department.
Home Care portion of HOSPICE might be handled with consultation from outside agencies such as Cook or Du Page County Department of Public Health.

ADVANTAGES OF RETAINING ACTIVITY

Home Health Aid Program will allow the hospital to provide service which currently is not provided in the community, but is much needed. The Home Care portion of HOSPICE is a significant part, especially if we do not develop a separate facility for a HOSPICE, but go with an in-house program for the dying patient.

CONSEQUENCES IF ACTIVITY IS ELIMINATED

Less than adequate home health services in this area because of consistent lack of home health aids.
Lack of effective follow-through for HOSPICE Program.

CASE EXAMPLE I

How the Director of Respiratory Care developed 19__ Departmental Objectives/Activities and how this eventually was related to the final Priority Ranking Form.

ALEXIAN BROTHERS MEDICAL CENTER

Department Name: Respiratory Care   19___   Departmental Objectives/Activities

(1) To provide acute ventilatory assistance to patients in respiratory failure—Code "99".

(2) To provide continuous ventilatory care to patients on ventilators in ICU and CCU or other units in the hospital (n.b., Nursery).

(3) To provide respiratory assistance in form of IPPB treatment to inpatients & outpatients with respiratory problems.

(4) To provide high humidity therapy in form of ultrasound or aerosol treatments to patients with respiratory congestion to help to clear the congestion.

(5) To provide chest physiotherapy to patients with chronic or acute respiratory congestion.

(6) To teach breathing exercises to chronic obstructive lung disease patients & walk with portable oxygen unit.

(7) To provide diagnostic procedures in form of arterial blood gases to help the physician to determine pulmonary gas exchange level in respiratory patients.

(8) To provide diagnostic procedure in form of pulmonary function studies to help the physicians to determine the extent of lung involvement in pulmonary disease cases.

(9) To provide necessary equipment as ordered by physician to patients with respiratory problems (ventilators, O_2 setups, croupettes, humidifiers).

(10) To maintain all equipment in functional order to provide patients with best possible means to deliver ordered therapy.

(11) To provide oxygen transports to patients who need O_2 continuously & have to go to other departments for diagnostic procedures.

(12) To provide supervision to personnel performing various functions. To provide inservice education to Dept's personnel & other departments in the hospital.

(13) To maintain patients' records according to JCAH standards, to maintain departmental records, process daily charges for services rendered, provide typed PF's reports.

(14) To attend educational seminars & meetings to update knowledge of new procedures & equipment in this field.

(15) To explore means for cost containment. To update departmental procedures as written in the manual.

(16) To provide respiratory assistance in home care programs as ordered by physician.

PRIORITY RANKING

Date ___August 30, 19___

DEPARTMENT	DIVISION	PREPARED	
Respiratory Care		APPROVED	PAGE 1 OF 1

RANK	ACTIVITY NAME AND DESCRIPTION	LEVEL	NO. OF NO.	CURRENT YEAR PER-SONNEL	CURRENT YEAR $ (000)	BUDGET YEAR PER-SONNEL	BUDGET YEAR $ (000)	BUDGET YEAR CUMULATIVE $ (000)
1	To Code "99"/providing acute ventilating assistance.	1	3	0.2	1,300	0.2	1,500	1,500
2	Continuous ventilatory care.	1	3	1.7	18,600	1.7	22,300	23,800
3	Blood gases.	1	3	1.0	10,690	1.1	14,500	38,300
4	Pulmonary function studies.	1	3	0.1	1,500	0.2	1,800	40,100
5	IPPB treatments.	2	3	8.9	94,700	8.9	113,700	153,800
6	Ultrasonic & aerosol treatments.	2	3	1.1	11,650	1.2	14,760	168,560
7	Chest physiotherapy.	2	3	1.0	10,690	1.0	13,090	181,650
8	Equipment setups & maintenance.	2	3	(−2.3) 1.5	14,650	4.2	52,550	234,200
9	Technical direction.	1	3	1.0	18,500	1.0	22,400	256,600
10	Supervision.	1	3	0.5	6,970	0.5	8,370	264,970
11	Secretarial function.	1	3	1.0	8,000	1.0	9,600	274,570
TOTALS				18.00	197,250	21.0	274,570	

CASE EXAMPLE J (TWO EXAMPLES)

How one department head, the Director of Pharmacy, created a *functional* organization chart as required for the first step of this process. Also, how complex the Respiratory Care *functional* organization chart turned out.

Case Example J (Part One)

Functional Organizational Chart—Pharmacy

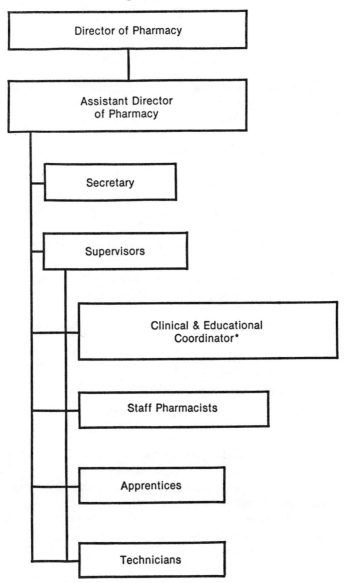

* Clinical & Educational Coordinator reports to Director and Assistant Director in this role and to Supervisors in the capacity of a Staff Pharmacist.

Functional Approach of Organizational Chart—Pharmacy

    I. Director of Pharmacy
   II. Assistant Director of Pharmacy (1.0 FTE) Responsible for:

      Scheduling
      Budgeting
      Purchasing of medications
      Review of incident reports
      Evaluation of employees
      Evaluation of products
      Nursing orientation presentation
      Hiring and firing of personnel

  III. Staff Supervisors (2.2 FTE) Responsible for:

      Evaluation of employees
      Evaluation of products
      Overall operation of designated areas of responsibility within the
        Pharmacy
      These two staff supervisors work opposing weekends, thus giving
        seven-day-per-week administrative coverage.

  IV. Clinical & Educational Coordinator (1.1 FTE) Responsible for:

      Pharmacy newsletter
      Diabetic talks on a group basis
      Diabetic talks on an individual basis
      Educating nursing personnel in IV medication classes
      Maintenance and upkeep of pharmaceutical library

   V. Secretary (1.0 FTE) Responsible for:

      Screening telephone calls to the assistant director and director
      Maintaining appointments and meetings
      Maintaining files
      Processing purchase orders
      Updating company order sheets
      Maintaining monthly reports
      Taking dictation of daily correspondence and monthly meetings

Pricing and processing doctors' charges
Greeting and assisting salesmen
Typing daily correspondence

VI. Staff Pharmacists (7.0 FTE) Responsible for:

Unit dose profiling
Unit does filling and checking
Preparation of primary IV's and IV piggybacks
Preparation of IV scheduling document
Preparation of IV labels
Filling and maintaining employee, outpatient, and emergency room
   prescriptions
Counseling of patients
Auditing of narcotics and alcohol
Preparation and dispensing of controlled alcohol

VII. Technicians (7.8 FTE) Responsible for:

Delivery of medication carts
Unit dose filling
Unit dose profiling
Replenishing of unit dose filling areas
Replenishing of center counter medications
Packaging of unit dose liquids & solids
Receiving of pharmaceutical merchandise
Aiding in preparation of primary IV's and IV piggybacks
Preparation and dispensing of individual and floor stock narcotic
   sheets
Aiding the pharmacists in filling and maintaining records of em-
   ployee, outpatient, and emergency room prescriptions
Replenishing of stock in outpatient pharmacy
Billing of requisitions, unit dose profiles, IV sheets, and blue no-
   charge requisitions.
Upkeep of price description master

VIII. Apprentices (2.4 FTE) Responsible for:

Apprentices are students who are attending Pharmacy School and
perform the same tasks as the technicians.

Case Example J (Part Two)

Functional Organizational Chart—Respiratory Care

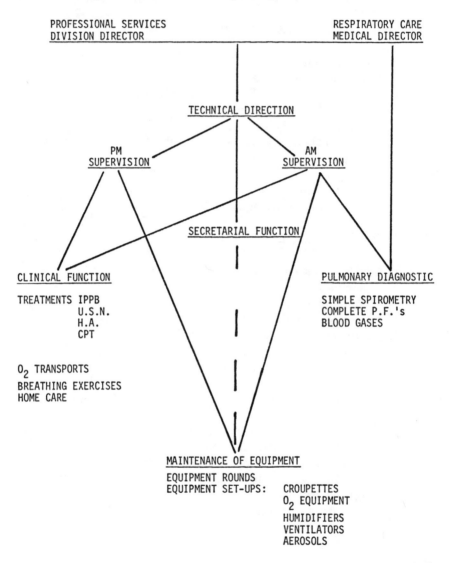

PROFESSIONAL SERVICES
DIVISION DIRECTOR

RESPIRATORY CARE
MEDICAL DIRECTOR

TECHNICAL DIRECTION

PM
SUPERVISION

AM
SUPERVISION

SECRETARIAL FUNCTION

CLINICAL FUNCTION

TREATMENTS IPPB
         U.S.N.
         H.A.
         CPT

O$_2$ TRANSPORTS
BREATHING EXERCISES
HOME CARE

PULMONARY DIAGNOSTIC

SIMPLE SPIROMETRY
COMPLETE P.F.'s
BLOOD GASES

MAINTENANCE OF EQUIPMENT

EQUIPMENT ROUNDS
EQUIPMENT SET-UPS: CROUPETTES
                     O$_2$ EQUIPMENT
                     HUMIDIFIERS
                     VENTILATORS
                     AEROSOLS

Exhibit A

ALEXIAN BROTHERS MEDICAL CENTER

Budget Year 19___ Departmental Objectives/Activities

Department Name: _____

(1) _____

(2) _____

(3) _____

(4) _____

(5) _____

(6) _____

(7) _____

(8) _____

(9) _____

(10) _____

(11) _____

(12) _____

(13) _____

(14) _____

(15) _____

(16) _____

Note: Departmental Objectives/Activities for upcoming fiscal year should relate to ABMC's overall One-Year Implementation Plan, departmental needs, and ranked in importance. The Division Director should review these objectives and rankings before proceeding with the zero-based budget decision packages.

Note: Departmental objectives should include continuance of fundamental "activities" or services, not just new programs or services.

EXHIBIT B

Alexian Brothers Medical Center

Instructions for Filling Out Decision Package (Exhibit C)

---

(1) Enter date submitted by initiating supervisor or manager.

(2) If Decision Package consists of (or relates to) an objective or current, fundamental activity included in Exhibit A, enter objective/activity identification number.

(3) Enter short title of the activity or departmental objective.

(4) Indicate level of effort. For example, if the Decision Package represents the "minimum" increment of a three-level activity, enter "level 1 of 3".

(5-6) Self-explanatory.

(7) Enter the signature (or initials) of the initiating supervisor/manager and of others in the approval chain. Generally, each Decision Package should be approved (with respect to correctness of information) by a department level executive.

(8) Enter Priority Ranking assigned to the Decision Package. Entry should be made in pencil to permit reranking at higher consolidation levels. Assign rank No. 1 to highest priority package.

(9) Describe the activity in terms of its purpose or intended result.

(10) Describe the activity in terms of the means or process by which the activity is to be accomplished.

(11) Where different ways of performing the activity have been evaluated, briefly describe the alternatives and the reasons why they were rejected. For example, if the Decision Package provides for the performance of a service in-house, why was the outside purchase rejected?

(12) State the principal benefits that will accrue to the hospital if the activity is retained (funded). Describe benefits to your own organization *and* other organizations that are affected.

(13) State the consequences that will result if the activity is eliminated (not funded). Distinguish between the consequences in your own organization and those in another organization.

(14-18) Fill in all applicable figures for budget year. If current year (expected) information is not readily available, provide reasonable estimate. To avoid misinterpretation, identify all data representing a partial year by indicating the number of months in parentheses. Round dollar figures to the nearest $100.

(14) Enter the number of employees (or equivalent employees) required to perform the activity.
(15) Enter the payroll costs of the activity.
(16) Enter the cost of major outside services, if any. Minor outside services should be included in No. 17.
(17) Enter the amount of other costs here.
(18) Total should equal the sum of No. 15, No. 16, and No. 17.

DECISION PACKAGE

Date _____

ACTIVITY (OR OBJECTIVE) NAME	DEPARTMENT	PREPARED	RANK

| LEVEL NO. _____ OF _____ | DIVISION | APPROVED | |

STATEMENT OF WORK OR PROGRAM

RESOURCES REQUIRED	CURRENT YEAR	BUDGET YEAR
Personnel		
Labor $		
Outside Services $		
Other $		
Total $		

ALTERNATIVE WAYS OF PERFORMING WORK OR PROGRAM AND COSTS

ADVANTAGES OF RETAINING ACTIVITY

CONSEQUENCES IF ACTIVITY IS ELIMINATED

EXHIBIT C

Decision Package

ACTIVITY/OBJECTIVE NO. _____ (2) _____   DATE _____ (1)

ACTIVITY (OR OBJECTIVE) NAME	DEPARTMENT (5)	PREPARED (7)	RANK (8)
(3) LEVEL NO. (4) OF	DIVISION (6)	APPROVED	

PURPOSE OF ACTIVITY (9)	RESOURCES REQUIRED	CURRENT YEAR	BUDGET YEAR
	PERSONNEL		(14)
	LABOR ($)		(15)
DESCRIPTION OF ACTIVITY (10)	OUTSIDE SERVICES ($)		(16)
	OTHER ($)		(17)
	TOTAL ($)		(18)

ALTERNATIVE WAYS OF PERFORMING WORK OR PROGRAM AND COSTS (11)

ADVANTAGES OF RETAINING ACTIVITY (12)

CONSEQUENCES IF ACTIVITY IS ELIMINATED (13)

PRIORITY RANKING

Date _____

DEPARTMENT	DIVISION	PREPARED	PAGE _____
		APPROVED	OF _____

RANK	ACTIVITY		CURRENT YEAR		BUDGET YEAR		
	NAME AND DESCRIPTION	LEVEL NO. OF NO.	PER-SONNEL	$ (000)	PER-SONNEL	$ (000)	CUMULA-TIVE $ (000)
TOTALS							

EXHIBIT D

Alexian Brothers Medical Center

Instructions for Filling Out Priority Ranking Form (Exhibit E)

(1) Enter date prepared by initiating supervisor or manager.

(2-3) Self-explanatory. "Division" should refer to the specific "cost center".

(4) Signature or initials of individual preparing the Ranking Form if other than the approving supervisor or manager.

(5) Signature or initials of supervisor or manager approving the Rankings shown on the form.

(6) Self-explanatory.

(7) Must agree with Ranking displayed on each Decision Package Form. First entry should be priority No. 1.

(8) Enter name of Activity from No. 3 of each Decision Package. If name is not sufficiently self-explanatory, underline name and add brief description summarized from No. 9 and No. 10 of the Decision Package.

(9) Package level number obtained from No. 4 of each Decision Package.

(10) Department Activity/Objective number, if applicable, obtained from No. 2 of each Decision Package obtained from Exhibit A.

(11-12) Personnel figures obtained from No. 14 of each Decision Package.

(13-14) Dollar figures obtained from No. 18 of each Decision Package.

(15) Enter cumulative total of budget year dollars.

(16-20) On each page of the Ranking Form, enter cumulative column totals as appropriate. Cumulative totals on last page will constitute grand totals.

EXHIBIT E Priority Ranking Form

RANK	ACTIVITY			CURRENT YEAR			BUDGET YEAR		
	NAME AND DESCRIPTION	LEVEL NO. OF NO.	ORG. OBJ. NO.	PERS.	$ (000)		PERS.	$ (000)	CULULA-TIVE $ (000)
(7)	(8)	(9)	(10)	(11)	(12)		(13)	(14)	(15)
TOTALS				(16)	(17)		(18)	(19)	(20)

PRIORITY RANKING FORM (3)

DEPARTMENT (2)   DIVISION   DATE ___ (1)

PREPARED (4)   PAGE ___ (6)

APPROVED (5)   OF ___

Index

NOTE: Zero-based budgeting is abbreviated ZBB throughout this index.

245

About the Author

Ray D. Dillon, D.B.A., C.P.A. is an Associate Professor of Accounting and Director of the undergraduate program in Business at Georgia State University in Atlanta. He has consulted with several allied health groups and health institutions. His articles have appeared in health care literature, business periodicals, and academic journals. He received an M.B.A. from Sam Houston State University and his doctorate from Texas Tech University. He resides in Avondale Estates, Georgia, with his wife, Sue, and son, Chris.